So Soft Bean Bag Teddy

The softest teddy bear you'll ever hold is quick to make. Create a collection in every color and fabric to keep in a basket in your home.

You can make this cuddle bear from all types of soft fabrics... mink-y fleece and chenille are especially good. Make one for a child's room, or attach one to a gift basket for someone in the hospital.

instructions on page 42

Mink-y fleece type fabrics are made from a new 100% polyester micro fiber.

Cuddle Bear Quilt

Shhh... Teddy is sleeping! What do you think he's dreaming about? Your toddler will look forward to nap time with this snuggle soft blankee and its friendly bear applique.

Add a ribbon bow near an ear to turn "him" into a "her" for your little girl.

instructions on pages 28 - 30

Headband, Poncho, Purse and Cap

Looking for fashionable attire for a blustery spring morning? Your little princess will love this warm and cozy poncho with its comfy cap. Made with pink and purple dot mink-y fleece and cute pink and yellow flowers, this feminine outfit is amazingly easy to construct and so quick to make, you'll have it finished in an afternoon.

Continue to accessorize with a heart-shaped purse with pretty Mink-y roses. While you are in your sewing room, why not make a matching poncho for yourself? Just make the square bigger, enlarge the head hole, and add a few more flowers.

instructions for cap and poncho pages 31 - 33, purse page 51 and headband 37

Springtime Pals Blankee and Flitterfly Puppet

Think Spring! This pastel hued blankee will bring a bit of springtime to your nursery or playroom any time of the year. It's the perfect stroller blanket to keep your little one cozy warm on those cool spring days.

This soft as the real thing butterfly will sit on your finger for as long as you want. When you wiggle your finger, the wings flap.

instructions on pages 19 - 24

Yipes Stripes Fringe Quilt and Bunny Doll

Check out this easy and interesting quilting technique! Fleece strips are tied and then hand stitched to the quilt top - so easy and so fast! And speaking of fast, strip piecing makes this blankee a lot easier to assemble than it looks!

You won't be able to stop making these blankees that combine the incredible softness of Mink-y with fun patterned fleeces. Polar fleece fringe softens the edge, giving your quilt a great finish.

instructions on pages 34 - 37

1. To make fringe, cut fleece into 1/2" strips just to the edge where they join the blankee.

Headband, Star Poncho, Cap and Burp Cloth

The headband has lovely rolled fleece roses that are very easy to make with just a few fiber scraps. In minutes you can make a dozen roses to use for all kinds of embellishments.

instructions on pages 31 - 33, 43

Looking for an easy to make baby gift that will really be appreciated? Every mother-to-be needs a collection of burp cloths. These small bits of luxury will pamper your newborn with exquisite softness. Make this small cloth with the leftover pieces from other projects in this book and you will be prepared for the next baby shower.

instructions on pages 31 - 33

Pillow and Bunny Doll

Add a splash of color to any room with this shabby-chic decorator pillow trimmed with beautiful lavender satin ribbon and charming green fringe. Then, continue the theme with this whimsical color-coordinated rabbit.

This bunny will nourish the imagination of your inner child and hop into your heart, bringing a smile to your face every time you look at it.

instructions on pages 60 and 36 - 37

Spots and Squares Quilt

"Wild thing, you make my heart sing. You make everything groovy."

Make your own Wild Thing Silly Bean doll with green fringe hair to charm today's heavy metal fan as well as yesterday's hard rock-and-roller.

Mink-y is not just for toddlers. Throw this colorful Dots Quilt over a chair in the music studio or family room and see if anyone can resist touching it.

Be warned – it won't be long before everyone wants one of their own.

instructions on pages 35 & 25

Silly Bean Dolls

Check out that hair and that goofy grin!

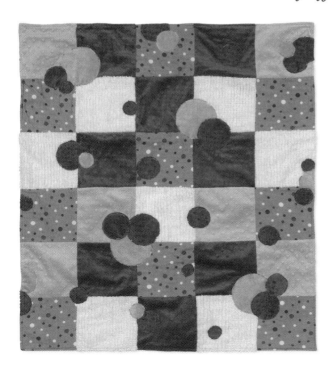

Bright colors, big eyes and a goofy grin make Silly Beans absolutely charismatic.

If you thought these projects were just for kids, set out a basket of them at the office and see what happens!

instructions on page 25

MAKING FRINGE

1. Determine the stretch direction of the fleece. Be sure to cut the fleece fringe so the stretchiest direction is on the long edge of the cut.

2. Pin the fringe to the bean.

Each darling animal has a part of their neck inside the fabric shirt, so your child can grip each one easily and pretend they are puppets.

MAKE A CAPE AND BODY

1. To make the body and cape, simply fold squares of Mink-y diagonally and snip 1/2" from tip. Layer the body and cape, insert neck and stitch in place.

Mink-y Pals

Who can resist this delightful collection of friends? Bunny Blue, Pink Kitty, Brown Bear and Yellow Ducky are all waiting to play or just cuddle up with your child.

instructions on page 40 - 41

Ducky Wrap and Toy

"Yellow Ducky, you're so fine. And I am so glad you're mine. Yellow Ducky, I'm so very fond of you.".

instructions on pages 38 - 39

Your child will love the flapping wings on this happy yellow duck. It's the perfect after-bath cuddle toy.

And be sure to treat your child to this pretty after-bath ducky wrap. It's snuggle soft and so much fun with the bath time fabric inside!

Yellow Ducky and the Wrap are also wonderful baby gifts.

instructions on pages 38 - 39

Cowboy Blankee

Ride 'em, Cowboy! Round up some nap time fun and lasso some dreams. This blankee will keep every little cowboy warm when he beds down for a nap. No actual quilting is needed.

instructions on pages 56 - 58

Ziggy Quilt and Pillows

Vroom! Start your imaginations. Piece the blue print fabric so it looks like a road. Your child's creativity will take over from there.

These fun car-shaped pillow toys will race through the paths on soft Mink-y Dots fabric, making all the needed sharp turns.

Car pillows are so soft they won't get injured when they collide! Tires are really fun add-ons when you sew two black circles of fabric together and add a smaller hubcap.

instructions on pages 44 - 47

Cube Toy and Froggy

Bright contrasting colors attract your eye to this fluffy Cube Toy, but once your hands get hold, you will find yourself playing catch or just enjoying its variety of textures.

Make this colorful block for the toddler in your life to help little ones learn colors, letters and numbers.

instructions on pages 48 - 49

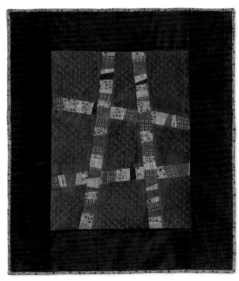

1. Cut Mink-y fabric strip in half lengthwise with a rotary cutter.

Headband, Kitty Poncho, Doll, and Burp Cloth

Make a sweet and soft headband that your little princess will love.

Then, complete her ensemble by adding the Mink-y poncho with a purr-fect heart pocket that holds a Mink-y kitty.

Use the scraps from this project to make a pretty burp cloth for a baby or your child's doll.

instructions on pages 52 - 53, 43 and 37

Jewel Tone Quilt

Simply gorgeous, this fun blankee is a great way to use those colorful flannel prints you have been collecting.

Rich jewel tone Mink-y Fleece complements the colors in the flannel perfectly.

Simple cut and sew methods promise great results!

instructions on page 50

HOW TO MAKE A MINK-Y ROSE

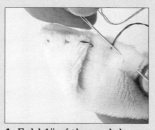

1. Fold 1" of the end down. Sew a Running stitch.

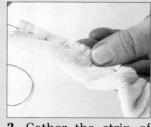

2. Gather the strip of fabric.

3. Roll the gathers into a rose and stitch to secure.

Three Bears and Pom-Poms Pillow

Re-enact the story of the *Three Bears* with these cuddly chenille toys and send your toddler off to dream in fairyland at nap time. You will enjoy making these fun characters as much as your child will love playing with them.

Do you need a pillow for your favorite storytelling chair? The textures of *Mink-y*, chenille, flannel and pom-poms work together beautifully in this gorgeous four-patch pillow. It is so easy to construct, you will have time to make a few.

instructions on page 54

Puffed Flowers Quilt

Large pink flowers do double duty on this very feminine spring-time quilt. The appliqued centers are quilted through all layers, providing a secure anchor while the dimensional flower adds style to the surface design.

This shabby chic blankee is sure to be the favorite for that special little girl in your life. Imagine the ooh's and ahh's you'll hear when you give this blankee at the baby shower!

instructions on page 55

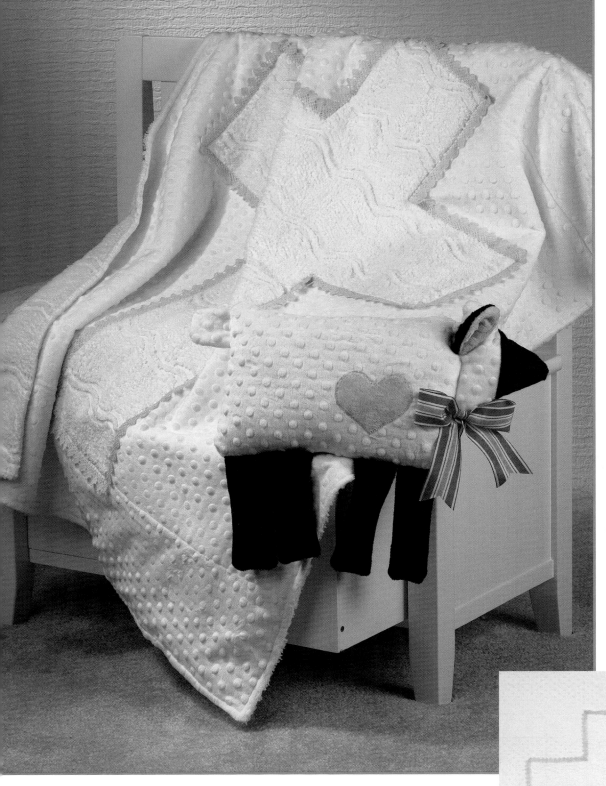

Lamb Pillow

Little Bo Peep may have lost her sheep, but your child will want to hang on to this soft-as-a-lamb pillow, especially at nap time.

Sweet dreams!

instructions on pages 26 - 27

Christening Blankee

For many, this is one of the most important days in a newborn's life. Celebrate a new baby's Christening day by making this special blankee that will be treasured for years to come.

instructions on page 59

Flitterfly Finger Puppet

FINISHED SIZE:
4½" x 5½"

FABRICS:
Mink-y Fleece:
   ⅛ yard Blue
   ⅛ yard Yellow

MATERIALS:
Purple embroidery
   floss
DMC Blue Pearl Cotton
   for antennae
8" ribbon ½" wide
Needle and thread

CUTTING:
2 Blue butterfly wings
   using pattern
2 Yellow butterfly
   bodies using pattern

INSTRUCTIONS:
All seam allowances
are ¼".

Wings:
   Pin wings right sides
together.
   Sew around the
edge, leaving a 2" open-
ing for turning.
   Clip curves. Turn
right sides out. Hand
stitch opening closed.

Body:
   Place body pieces
right sides together.
   Sew around the
edge, leaving a 2" open-
ing for turning.
   Clip curves. Turn
right sides out.
   Hand stitch opening
closed.

Assembly:
   Center body on
wings. Hand stitch in
place along the edges
where the body meets
the wings.
   The space between
the body and the wings
is where your finger
slides in.

Finish:
   Embroider eyes and
antennae.
   Stitch ribbon at the
neck, tie into a bow.

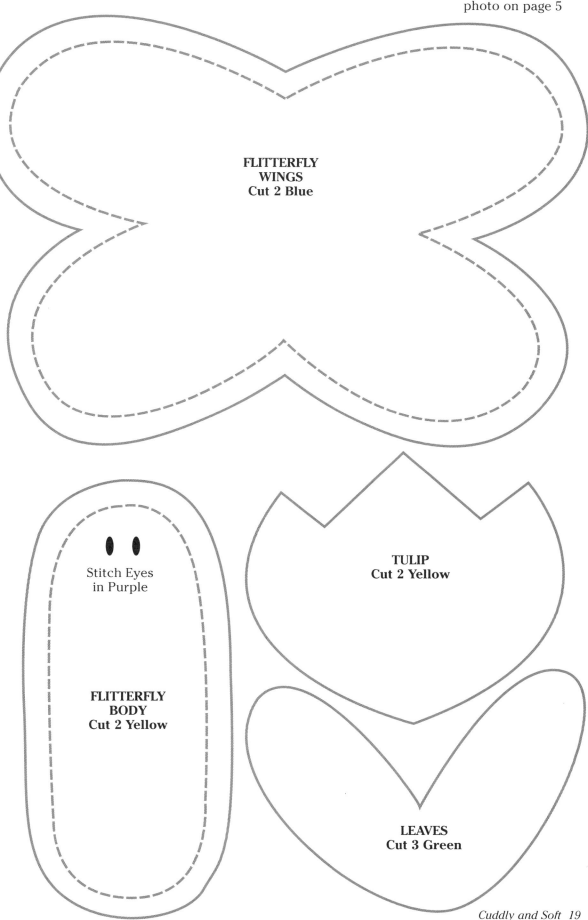

FLITTERFLY
WINGS
Cut 2 Blue

Stitch Eyes
in Purple

FLITTERFLY
BODY
Cut 2 Yellow

TULIP
Cut 2 Yellow

LEAVES
Cut 3 Green

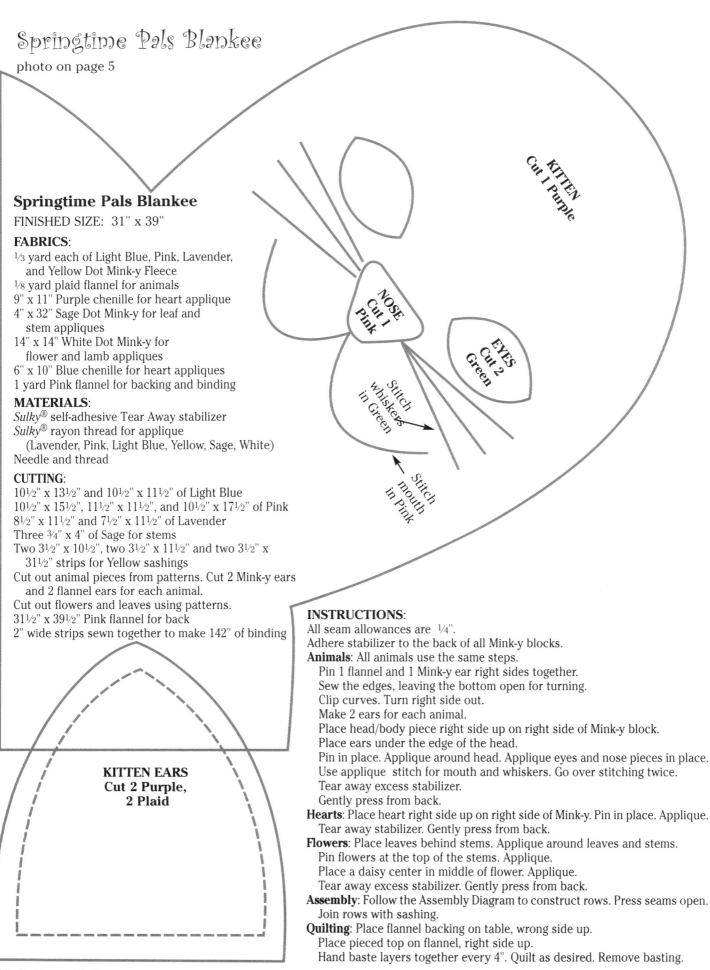

Springtime Pals Blankee

photo on page 5

KITTEN
Cut 1 Purple

NOSE
Cut 1
Pink

EYES
Cut 2
Green

Stitch
whiskers
in Green

Stitch
mouth
in Pink

Springtime Pals Blankee

FINISHED SIZE: 31" x 39"

FABRICS:
⅓ yard each of Light Blue, Pink, Lavender,
    and Yellow Dot Mink-y Fleece
⅛ yard plaid flannel for animals
9" x 11" Purple chenille for heart applique
4" x 32" Sage Dot Mink-y for leaf and
    stem appliques
14" x 14" White Dot Mink-y for
    flower and lamb appliques
6" x 10" Blue chenille for heart appliques
1 yard Pink flannel for backing and binding

MATERIALS:
Sulky® self-adhesive Tear Away stabilizer
Sulky® rayon thread for applique
    (Lavender, Pink, Light Blue, Yellow, Sage, White)
Needle and thread

CUTTING:
10½" x 13½" and 10½" x 11½" of Light Blue
10½" x 15½", 11½" x 11½", and 10½" x 17½" of Pink
8½" x 11½" and 7½" x 11½" of Lavender
Three ¾" x 4" of Sage for stems
Two 3½" x 10½", two 3½" x 11½" and two 3½" x
    31½" strips for Yellow sashings
Cut out animal pieces from patterns. Cut 2 Mink-y ears
    and 2 flannel ears for each animal.
Cut out flowers and leaves using patterns.
31½" x 39½" Pink flannel for back
2" wide strips sewn together to make 142" of binding

KITTEN EARS
Cut 2 Purple,
2 Plaid

INSTRUCTIONS:
All seam allowances are ¼".
Adhere stabilizer to the back of all Mink-y blocks.
Animals: All animals use the same steps.
    Pin 1 flannel and 1 Mink-y ear right sides together.
    Sew the edges, leaving the bottom open for turning.
    Clip curves. Turn right side out.
    Make 2 ears for each animal.
    Place head/body piece right side up on right side of Mink-y block.
    Place ears under the edge of the head.
    Pin in place. Applique around head. Applique eyes and nose pieces in place.
    Use applique stitch for mouth and whiskers. Go over stitching twice.
    Tear away excess stabilizer.
    Gently press from back.
Hearts: Place heart right side up on right side of Mink-y. Pin in place. Applique.
    Tear away stabilizer. Gently press from back.
Flowers: Place leaves behind stems. Applique around leaves and stems.
    Pin flowers at the top of the stems. Applique.
    Place a daisy center in middle of flower. Applique.
    Tear away excess stabilizer. Gently press from back.
Assembly: Follow the Assembly Diagram to construct rows. Press seams open.
    Join rows with sashing.
Quilting: Place flannel backing on table, wrong side up.
    Place pieced top on flannel, right side up.
    Hand baste layers together every 4". Quilt as desired. Remove basting.

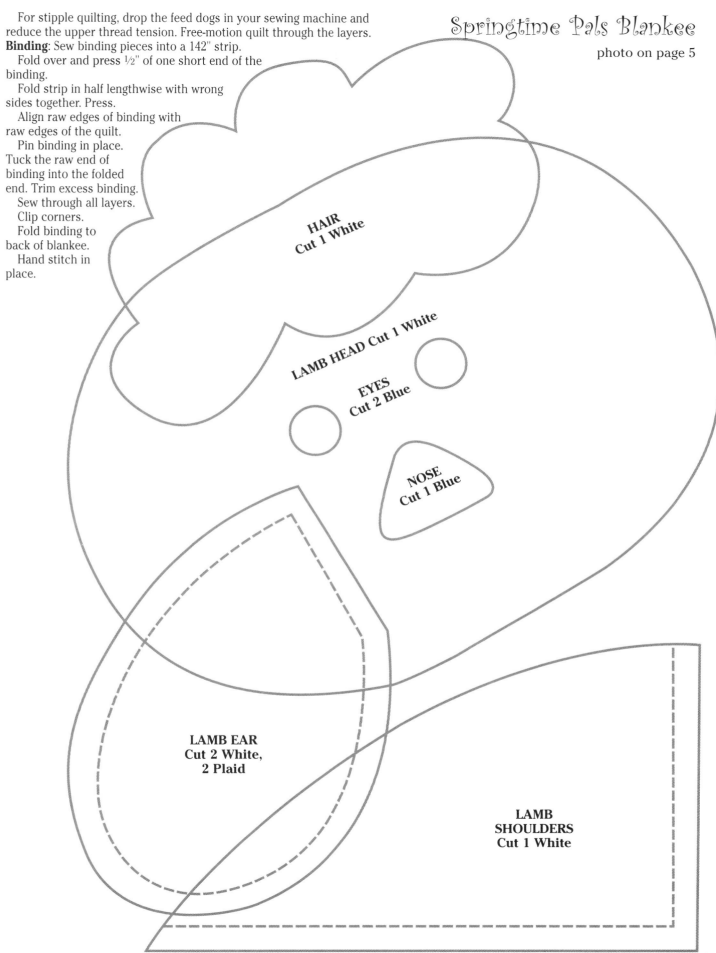

For stipple quilting, drop the feed dogs in your sewing machine and reduce the upper thread tension. Free-motion quilt through the layers.

Binding: Sew binding pieces into a 142" strip.

Fold over and press ½" of one short end of the binding.

Fold strip in half lengthwise with wrong sides together. Press.

Align raw edges of binding with raw edges of the quilt.

Pin binding in place. Tuck the raw end of binding into the folded end. Trim excess binding.

Sew through all layers.

Clip corners.

Fold binding to back of blankee.

Hand stitch in place.

HAIR
Cut 1 White

LAMB HEAD Cut 1 White

EYES
Cut 2 Blue

NOSE
Cut 1 Blue

LAMB EAR
Cut 2 White,
2 Plaid

LAMB
SHOULDERS
Cut 1 White

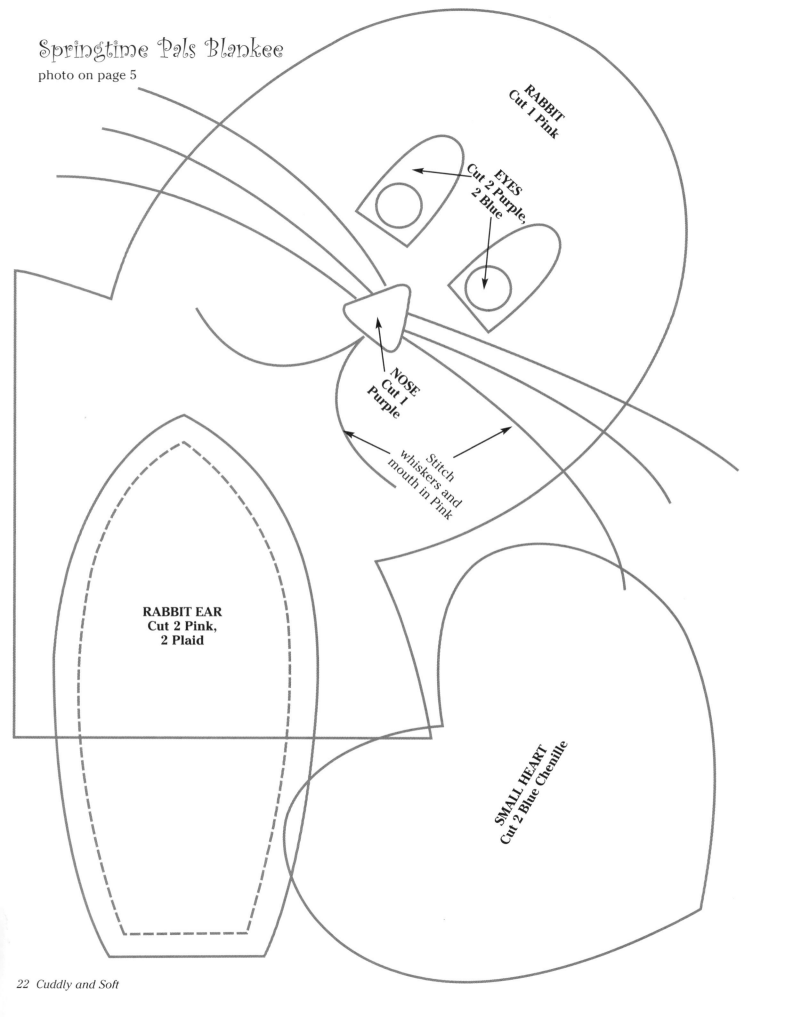

Springtime Pals Blankee
photo on page 5

RABBIT
Cut 1 Pink

EYES
Cut 2 Purple,
2 Blue

NOSE
Cut 1
Purple

Stitch
whiskers and
mouth in Pink

RABBIT EAR
Cut 2 Pink,
2 Plaid

SMALL HEART
Cut 2 Blue Chenille

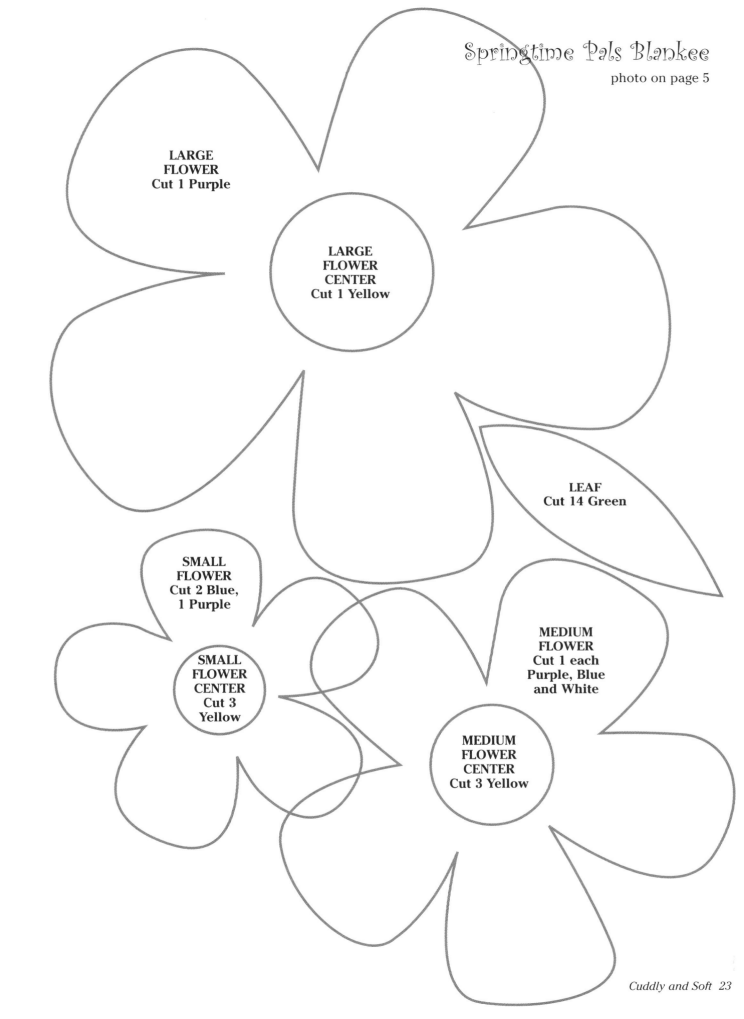

**LARGE
FLOWER
Cut 1 Purple**

**LARGE
FLOWER
CENTER
Cut 1 Yellow**

**LEAF
Cut 14 Green**

**SMALL
FLOWER
Cut 2 Blue,
1 Purple**

**SMALL
FLOWER
CENTER
Cut 3
Yellow**

**MEDIUM
FLOWER
Cut 1 each
Purple, Blue
and White**

**MEDIUM
FLOWER
CENTER
Cut 3 Yellow**

Springtime Pals Blankee
photo on page 5

LARGE HEART
Cut 1 purple

Assembly Diagram for
Springtime Pals Blankee

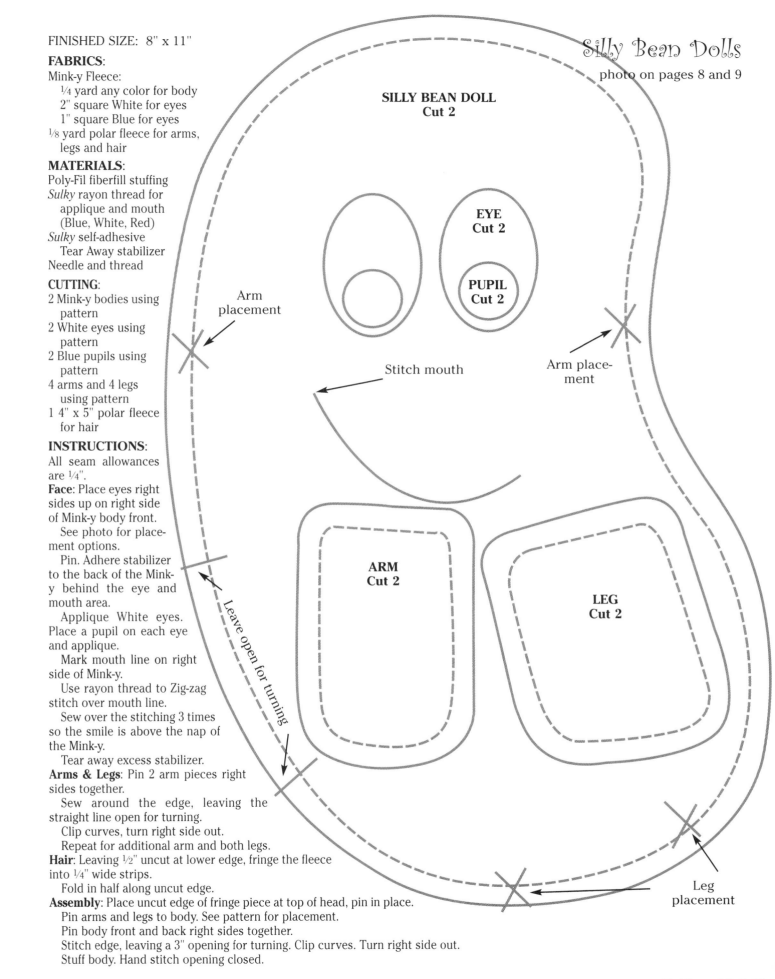

FINISHED SIZE: 8" x 11"

FABRICS:
Mink-y Fleece:
¼ yard any color for body
2" square White for eyes
1" square Blue for eyes
⅛ yard polar fleece for arms,
legs and hair

MATERIALS:
Poly-Fil fiberfill stuffing
Sulky rayon thread for
applique and mouth
(Blue, White, Red)
Sulky self-adhesive
Tear Away stabilizer
Needle and thread

CUTTING:
2 Mink-y bodies using
pattern
2 White eyes using
pattern
2 Blue pupils using
pattern
4 arms and 4 legs
using pattern
1 4" x 5" polar fleece
for hair

INSTRUCTIONS:
All seam allowances
are ¼".
Face: Place eyes right
sides up on right side
of Mink-y body front.
See photo for place-
ment options.
Pin. Adhere stabilizer
to the back of the Mink-
y behind the eye and
mouth area.
Applique White eyes.
Place a pupil on each eye
and applique.
Mark mouth line on right
side of Mink-y.
Use rayon thread to Zig-zag
stitch over mouth line.
Sew over the stitching 3 times
so the smile is above the nap of
the Mink-y.
Tear away excess stabilizer.
Arms & Legs: Pin 2 arm pieces right
sides together.
Sew around the edge, leaving the
straight line open for turning.
Clip curves, turn right side out.
Repeat for additional arm and both legs.
Hair: Leaving ½" uncut at lower edge, fringe the fleece
into ¼" wide strips.
Fold in half along uncut edge.
Assembly: Place uncut edge of fringe piece at top of head, pin in place.
Pin arms and legs to body. See pattern for placement.
Pin body front and back right sides together.
Stitch edge, leaving a 3" opening for turning. Clip curves. Turn right side out.
Stuff body. Hand stitch opening closed.

SILLY BEAN DOLL
Cut 2

EYE
Cut 2

PUPIL
Cut 2

Arm
placement

Arm place-
ment

Stitch mouth

Leave open for turning

ARM
Cut 2

LEG
Cut 2

Leg
placement

Lamb Pillow

photo on page 18

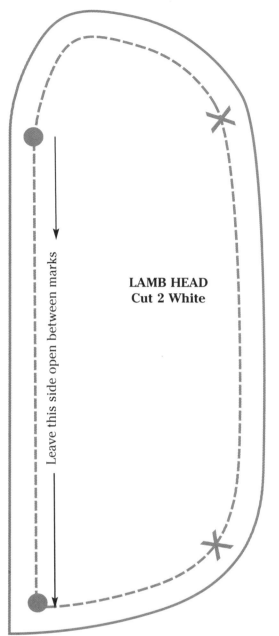

LAMB HEAD
Cut 2 White

Leave this side open between marks

Lamb Pillow

FINISHED SIZE: 12" x 16"

FABRICS:
Mink-y Fleece:
  1/4 yard White Dots
  1/8 yard Black
  1/8 yard Pink

MATERIALS:
Poly-Fil fiberfill stuffing
Sulky Pink rayon thread for applique
Sulky self-adhesive Tear Away stabilizer
15" ribbon 1 1/2" wide
Needle and thread

CUTTING:
8 leg pieces 1 1/2" x 5" and 2 faces from Black Mink-y
2 ears each from Black and Pink Mink-y
2 bodies 8" x 11", 2 heads and 2 tails from White Mink-y
1 heart from Pink Mink-y

INSTRUCTIONS:
All seam allowances are 1/4".

Legs: For each leg, place 2 pieces of Mink-y right sides together.
  Stitch 3 sides leaving one end open. Clip corners, turn right sides out

Ears: Place one Black and one Pink ear right sides together. Stitch sides, leaving bottom open.
  Clip curves, turn right sides out.
  Fold ears in half, with Pink Mink-y to the inside.
  Stitch along open edge to secure.

Tail: Place right sides together, stitching the edges and leaving the straight side open.
  Clip curves. Turn right sides out.

Face: Pin face to head right sides together, lining up between X marks. Stitch face to head. Repeat for other side.

Head: Place face/head pieces right sides together. Stitch, leaving open between large dots. Clip curves. Turn right sides out.
  Use Poly-Fil to stuff face & head to medium firmness.

Body: Pin heart on body, as shown.
  Adhere 4" square of stabilizer on wrong side of Mink-y behind the heart.
  Applique heart in place. Remove excess stabilizer.
  Following the placement diagram, pin legs, tail, ears, and head on the right side of one body piece.
  Place second body piece on top, right sides together.
  Beginning below the ear, stitch all layers together continuing around to 2" before the head.
  Clip curves. Turn right sides out. Stuff body.
  Stitch opening closed, securing head and ears in place.
  Make a ribbon bow and stitch it to the neck.

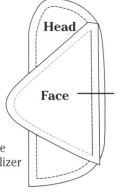

Head

Face

Sew 1 face and 1 head piece, right sides together, then sew the other face and head piece, right sides together leaving open between dots for stuffing.

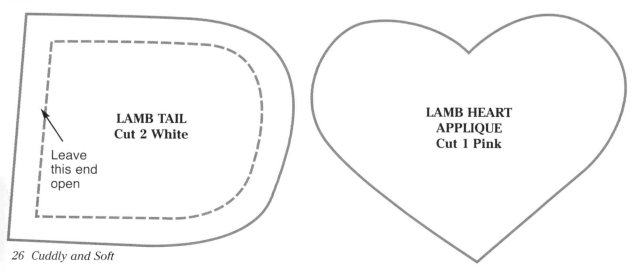

LAMB TAIL
Cut 2 White

Leave this end open

LAMB HEART
APPLIQUE
Cut 1 Pink

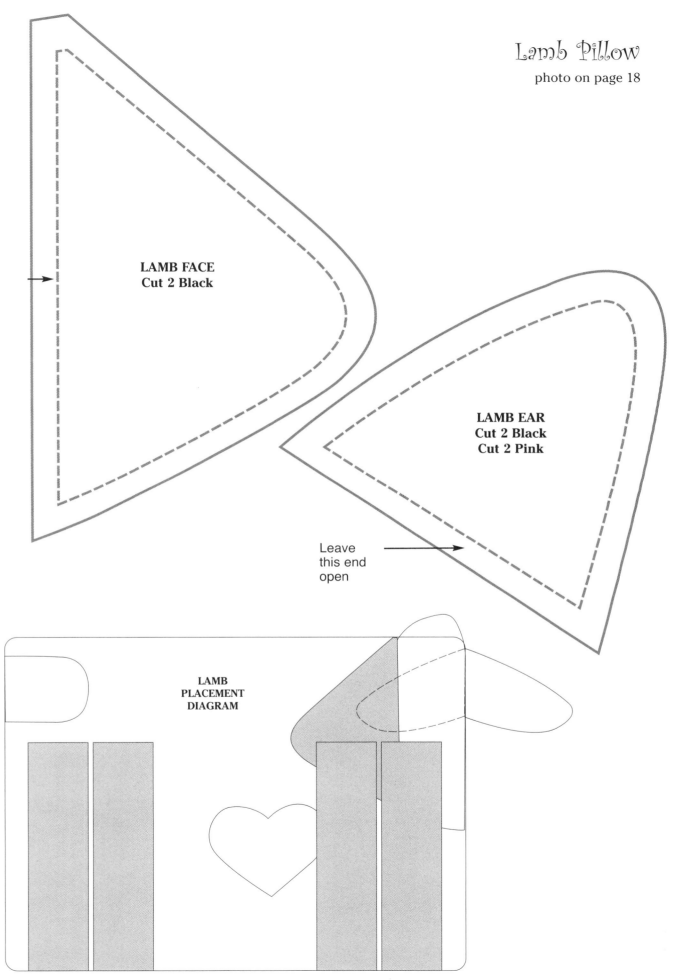

Lamb Pillow
photo on page 18

LAMB FACE
Cut 2 Black

LAMB EAR
Cut 2 Black
Cut 2 Pink

Leave
this end
open

LAMB
PLACEMENT
DIAGRAM

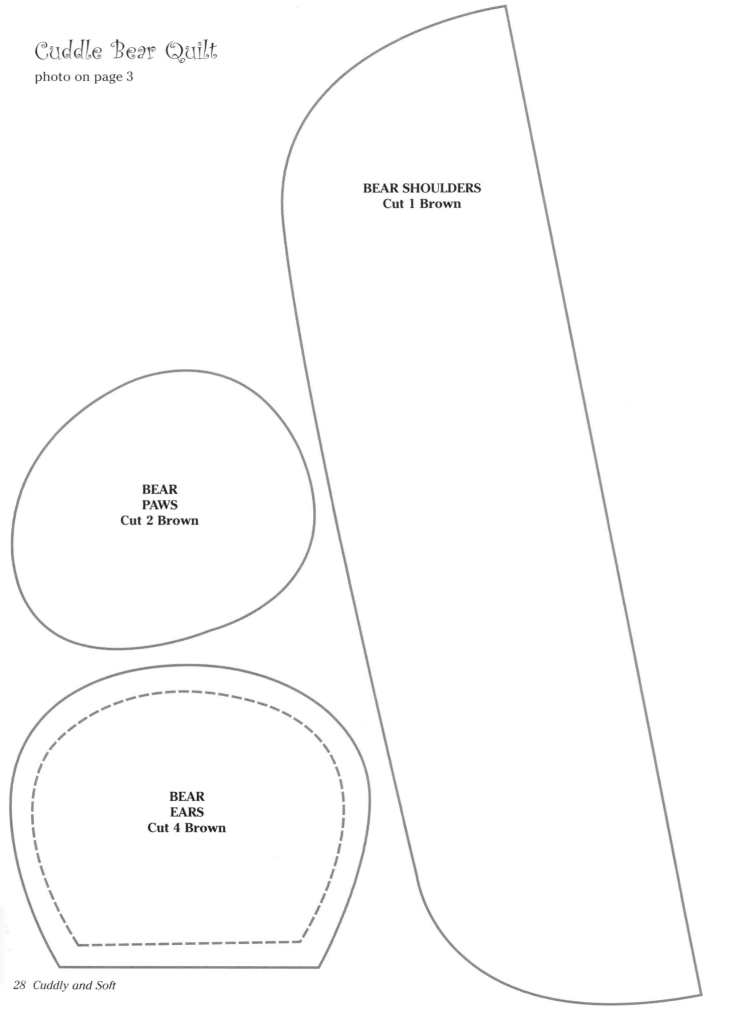

Cuddle Bear Quilt
photo on page 3

BEAR SHOULDERS
Cut 1 Brown

**BEAR
PAWS
Cut 2 Brown**

**BEAR
EARS
Cut 4 Brown**

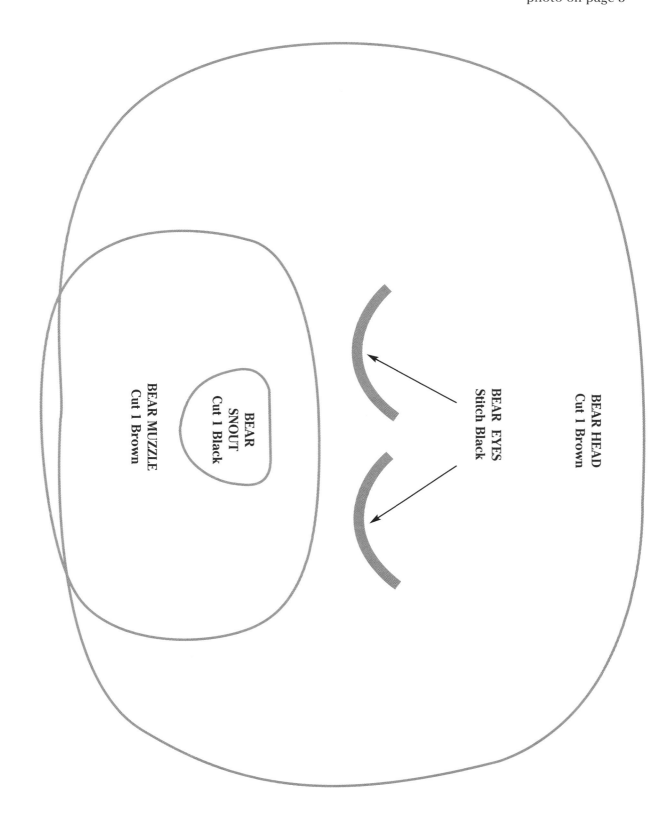

BEAR HEAD
Cut 1 Brown

BEAR EYES
Stitch Black

BEAR MUZZLE
Cut 1 Brown

BEAR
SNOUT
Cut 1 Black

Cuddle Bear Quilt

photo on page 3

CUDDLE BEAR ASSEMBLY DIAGRAM

FINISHED SIZE: 30" x 31"

FABRICS:
Mink-y Fleece:
  ¾ yard Dark Brown Dot
  ⅝ yard Peach
  ⅛ yard Pink Dot
  ¼ yard Light Brown
  3" square Black

MATERIALS:
Sulky self-adhesive Tear Away stabilizer,
Sulky rayon thread for applique (Black, Light Brown)
2 yards grosgrain ribbon 1½" wide
Needle and thread

CUTTING:
18½" x 31½" Peach Mink-y
15" square stabilizer
From Light Brown Mink-y, cut shoulder, head, muzzle, 2 paws, 4 ears.
From Black Mink-y, cut nose and 2 sleeping eyes
3½" x 18½" Pink Dot
Two 6½" x 31½" Dark Brown Dot side borders
30½" x 31½" Dark Brown Dot backing
2½" wide strips of Dark Brown sewn together to make 124" of binding

INSTRUCTIONS:
All seam allowances are ¼".

Bear:
   Adhere stabilizer 3" below the top edge on the back of the Peach Mink-y.
   Center the bear shoulder 10" from the top. Applique shoulder in place.

Ears:
Pin 2 ear pieces right sides together. Sew together, leaving the bottom edge open for turning.
   Clip curves. Turn right side out.
   Make second ear.
   Place bear head right side up on Peach Mink-y, overlapping the shoulder piece.
   Place ears under the head piece. Pin ears and head in place.
   Applique around the head.

Face:
   Applique muzzle and nose in place.
   For sleeping eyes, applique stitch twice over the center of the eye piece.

Finish:
   Align Pink Dot rectangle along the lower edge of the shoulder piece, right sides together.
   Pin in place. Sew the long edge.
   Flip Pink Mink-y piece right side up. Turn under ¼" of raw edge of Pink Mink-y.
   Pin to Peach Mink-y. Zig-zag along the edge to secure. Pin and applique paws in place.
   Tear away excess stabilizer. From wrong side, lightly press appliqued bear.

Assembly:
   Pin side borders and sew in place. Press seams open.
   Cut ribbons the same length as the long seam.
   Center a ribbon over each seam. Pin. Sew closely to both edges of the ribbons. Press lightly.

Finishing: Layer backing and blankee top wrong sides together.

Binding:
   Join strips together at angles to reduce bulk.
   Fold one end down ½". Fold binding in half lengthwise, wrong sides together.
   Align raw edges of binding with raw edges of quilt.
   Tuck the raw end into the folded end. Pin and sew binding.
   Fold binding to back. Hand stitch in place.

FINISHED SIZE: 10" tall, 17" around the opening

FABRICS:
Mink-y Fleece:
    ⅓ yard Lavender
    ⅓ yard Light Blue
    ⅛ yard Pink
    ⅛ yard Pale Yellow

MATERIALS:
Sulky rayon thread for applique (Pink, Lavender, Pale Yellow)
Sulky self-adhesive Tear Away stabilizer
Needle and thread

CUTTING:
10" x 20" Lavender Mink-y Fleece
10" x 20" Light Blue Mink-y Fleece
7 Pink Mink-y flowers using pattern
6 Yellow Mink-y flower centers using pattern
7 Lavender Mink-y stars using pattern

INSTRUCTIONS:
All seam allowances are ¼".

Flowers:
    Place Lavender Mink-y right side up.
    Place 5 flowers right sides up on Mink-y, 2" down from upper long edge.
    Pin in place. Adhere a 4" square of stabilizer behind pinned flowers.
    Use rayon thread to applique in place.
    Place centers in flowers. Applique. Remove excess stabilizer.
    Gently press flowers from wrong side.

Stars:
    Place Blue Mink-y right side up.
    Place 5 stars right sides up on Mink-y, 2" down from upper long edge.
    Pin in place. Adhere a 4" square of stabilizer behind pinned stars.
    Use rayon thread to applique.
    Remove excess stabilizer. Gently press stars from wrong side.

Assembly:
    Place appliqued Mink-y pieces right sides together.
    Pin the long edge opposite the appliques. Sew the long edge.
    Open the fabric with right sides facing you.
    See diagram to refold with right sides together forming a tube. Sew.
    Fold the tube inside itself so the right sides are out.
    Topstitch ¼" from the folded/sewn edge.
    Hand gather the raw edges at the top separately using doubled thread and
running stitches.
    Gather tightly, secure thread.
    Stitch through both gathered layers to secure both hat layers to one another.

Finishing:
    Hat is topped on one side by a flower, on the other side by a star.
    Place 2 flower pieces right sides together.
    Stitch all around. Clip curves and corners. Make small slit in one layer of flower.
    Turn right sides out. Place a flower center in middle over the slit. Applique in place.
    Hand sew to the top of the hat.
    Repeat for a star on the other side.

    HAT SIZES AND HEAD CIRCUMFERENCE:
        Small: 0-6 months, 16";
        Medium: 6-12 months, 17";
        Large: 12-18 months, 18";
        Extra Large: 18-24 months, 19".
Add 2" to head measurements to allow
for seam allowances and fabric thickness.

patterns are on page 32 - 33

Assembly Diagram

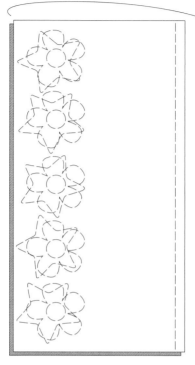

1. With right sides together, sew the seam opposite the appliques.

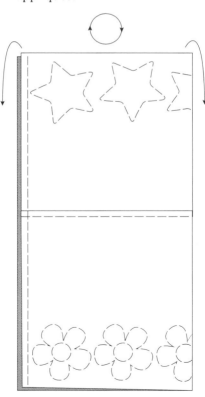

3. Fold the tube in on itself. Topstitch this seam.

2. Open and refold. Sew long edge.

Reversible Poncho (Flowers on one side, Stars on the other)

photo on pages 4 and 7

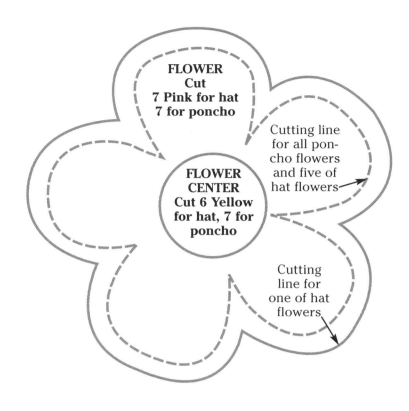

FLOWER
Cut
7 Pink for hat
7 for poncho

FLOWER CENTER
Cut 6 Yellow for hat, 7 for poncho

Cutting line for all poncho flowers and five of hat flowers

Cutting line for one of hat flowers

STAR
Cut 6 Lavender for poncho, 7 for hat

Cutting line for all poncho stars and five of hat stars

Cutting line for one of hat stars

FINISHED SIZE: 24" x 24"

FABRICS:
Mink-y Fleece:
⅔ yard Lavender Dot
⅔ yard Light Blue Dot
¼ yard Pink Dot
⅛ yard Light Yellow
⅛ yard Sage Green

MATERIALS:
Sulky rayon thread for applique
(Pink, Sage, Lavender, Pale Yellow)
Sulky self-adhesive Tear Away stabilizer
Needle and thread

CUTTING:
18½" square each of Lavender and Blue
3½" x 18½" Two each of Pink and Lavender
3½" x 24½" Two each of Pink and Lavender
2½" x 24" strip of Lavender for neck binding
7 Pink flowers using pattern
7 Sage leaves using pattern
7 Yellow flower centers using pattern
6 Lavender stars using pattern

INSTRUCTIONS:
All seam allowances are ¼".
Poncho:
Place one short Pink strip right sides together with the Lavender square.
Stitch together on long edge. Repeat for opposite edge.
Stitch long strips to remaining edges. Gently press seams open.
Place one short Lavender strip right sides together with the Blue square.
Stitch together on long edge. Repeat for opposite edge.
Stitch long strips to remaining edges. Gently press seams open.
Applique:
Place leaves as desired on right side of poncho.
Pin in place.
Adhere 4" squares of stabilizer on wrong side of Mink-y behind pinned leaves.
Use rayon thread to applique.
Place flowers on leaves and applique.
Position flower centers and applique.
Tear away stabilizer. Gently press from wrong side.
Repeat for stars on the Blue square.
Assembly:
Place poncho right sides together. Pin.
Sew around the edge leaving a 6" opening for turning.
Clip corners. Turn right side out. Gently press edge.
Hand stitch opening closed. Topstitch ¼" from the edge.
Cut neck hole opening in center through both layers.
Neck binding:
Fold under ½" of one short end of the 2½" x 24" strip.
Fold in half lengthwise.
Pin raw edges of binding to raw edges of hole in poncho.
Trim excess.
Tuck raw end into folded end, trim excess.
Stitch all around.
Fold binding to other side of poncho. Hand stitch to secure.

Reversible Poncho (Flowers on one side, Stars on the other)

photo on pages 4 and 7

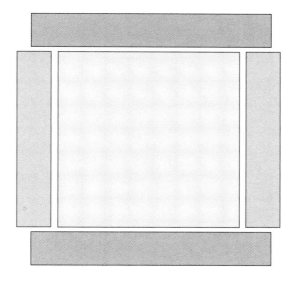

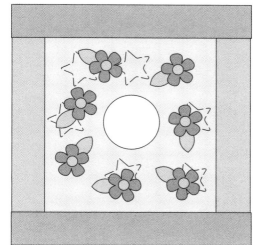

Assembly Diagram for Poncho

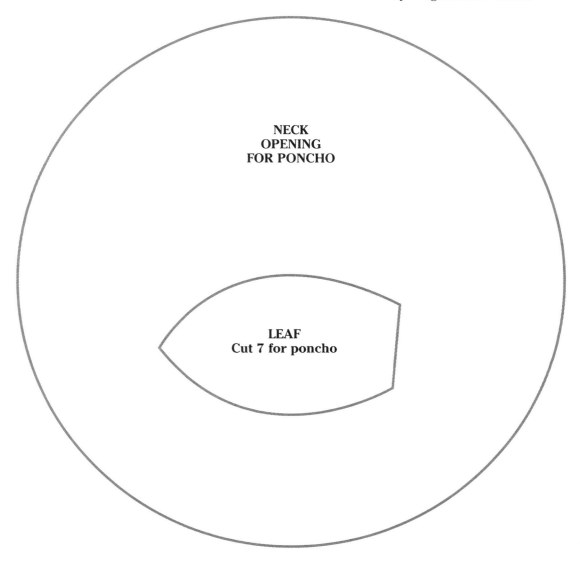

**NECK
OPENING
FOR PONCHO**

**LEAF
Cut 7 for poncho**

Yipes Stripes Fringe Quilt

photo on page 6

A = Yellow Dot
B = Polar Fleece
C = Sage Dot
D = Lavender Chenille

Yipes Stripes Rail Fence Blankee

FINISHED SIZE: 30" x 40"

FABRICS:
Mink-y Fleece
⅓ yard of Yellow Dot
⅓ yard of Sage Dot
1 yard of polar fleece
½ yard Lavender chenille
1¼ yard of Sage flannel for back

MATERIALS:
Needle and thread

CUTTING:
Four 3" x 32" strips from each Mink-y Fleece, Polar fleece
    and chenille
One 30½" x 40½" Sage flannel for backing
Forty-two ½" x 4" polar fleece strips for quilting
Fringe:
    Determine the stretch direction of the fleece.
    Be sure to cut fleece so the stretchiest direction is
on the long edge of the pieces you will cut.
    From fleece, cut 2 pieces measuring 4" x 40"
and one piece measuring 4" x 30".

INSTRUCTIONS:
All seam allowances are ¼".
Strip Piecing:
    Sew strips together in the following order:
    Yellow Dots, polar fleece, Sage Dots, Lavender chenille.
    Cut the strip into twelve 10½" blocks.
Assembling top:
    See Assembly Diagram.
    For each row, stitch 3 blocks together.
    Make 4 rows. Press seam allowances open.
    Stitch rows together on long edge. Press seam allowances open.
Fringe:
    Place pieced top right side up on table.
    Place fleece strips right sides together on 3 edges of pieced top.
    Pin securely. Baste if desired.
Backing:
    Place the backing on the pieced top and fleece with right sides
together.
    Pin all layers.
    Stitch through all layers around the perimeter, leaving an 8"
opening for turning.
    Clip the corners. Turn right side out. Hand stitch the opening
closed.
    Gently press edges.
    Topstitch ¼" all around edge.
Cutting Fringe:
    To fringe the edges, cut fleece into ½" strips,
cutting just to the edge where they join the blankee.
Finishing:
    Tie a knot in the center of each fleece quilting strip.
    Place on blankee top as desired.
    Hand stitch each knot to blankee through all layers.

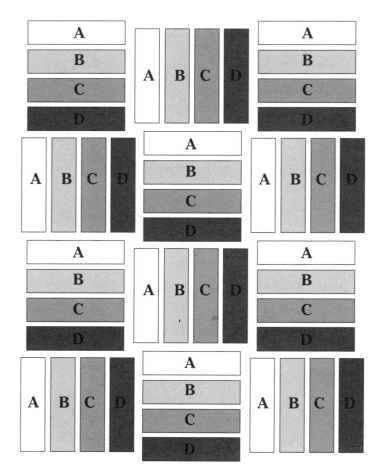

Assembly Diagram

Assembly Diagram

Spots and Squares Quilt

FINISHED SIZE: 30" x 36"

FABRICS:

Mink-y Fleece:

⅓ yard Purple

⅓ yard Light Blue

Assorted Orange, Fuchsia, and Purple scraps for circle appliques

½ yard Yellow chenille

1 yard of Blue Dot flannel for squares and back

MATERIALS:

Sulky variegated rayon thread for appliques

Needle and thread

CUTTING:

6½" blocks:

9 Blue Dot flannel

7 Yellow chenille

8 Purple Mink-y

6 Light Blue Mink-y

30½" x 36½" from Blue Dot flannel for backing

Circles for Appliques:

Orange: Four 4", Two 2½" (cut one in half), Three 1½"

Fuchsia: Two 3½"; Three 3", One 2¾", Two 2½", Four 2¼";
   Three 1¾", Five 1¼"

Purple: Two 2¼"; One 2½", One 3"

INSTRUCTIONS:

All seam allowances are ¼".

Assembly:

Follow the Assembly Diagram to make 6 rows, 5 blocks each.

Sew the rows together. Press seam allowances open.

Backing:

Place the backing on the pieced top with right sides together.

Pin all layers.

Sew through all layers around the perimeter, leaving an 8" opening for turning.

Clip the corners. Turn right side out. Hand stitch opening closed. Gently press edges.

Topstitch ¼" all around edge.

Finishing:

Position circles for applique according to the Assembly Diagram or as desired.

Pin in place.

Applique through all layers with variegated thread.

4"

3½"

3"

2¾"

2½"

2¼"

1¾"

1½"

1¼"

A = Blue Dot flannel

B = Yellow chenille

C = Purple Mink-y

D = Light Blue Mink-y

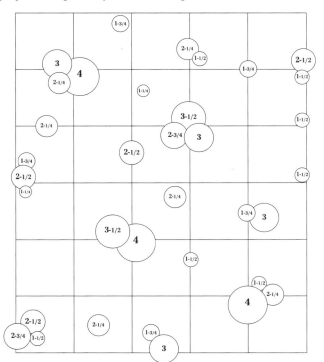

Assembly Diagram

A	B	C	B	A
D	C	A	C	D
A	D	B	D	A
B	C	A	C	B
A	B	C	B	A
D	C	A	C	D

Bunny Doll

FINISHED SIZE:
12" (not including ears)

FABRICS:
1/3 yard Lavender Mink-y Fleece
1/3 yard Lavender chenille
1/3 yard flannel

MATERIALS:
15" ribbon 5/8" wide
Black and Pink embroidery floss
   for face
Poly-Fil polyester stuffing or
   stuffing pellets
Needle and thread

CUTTING:
2 ears from Mink-y
2 ears from flannel
1 head from Mink-y
1 head from flannel or chenille
1 bunny front right from flannel or chenille
1 bunny front left from Mink-y or chenille
1 right back and left back bunny of chenille,
Mink-y or flannel

INSTRUCTIONS:
All seam allowances are 1/4".
Ears: For each ear, place a Mink-y and a flannel piece right sides together.
   Stitch sides leaving the straight edge open for turning.
      Clip curves. Turn right sides out.
         Body: Pin and sew left and right pieces along center seam. Press seam open.
            Pin head to top of body front. Sew across neck. Press seam open.
            Place ears, right sides together, at top of head. Baste in place.
            Place body front and back right sides together. Pin all around.
            Sew front to back starting next to ear, leaving the top of the head open for turning.
            Clip curves, turn right side out.
            Lightly stuff arms and legs.
            Sew across limbs, as indicated on the pattern to create jointed limbs.
            Firmly stuff body, neck and head. Hand stitch the top of the head closed.
   Finishing: Use embroidery floss to embroider face.
            Start the thread in the middle of the eye or nose.
            Cover the knot with Satin stitches.
            Tie a ribbon bow around neck.

BUNNY BODY
Flip pattern for each side of body and cut 2 fronts and 2 backs

Ear placement

BUNNY HEAD
Cut 1 front and 1 back

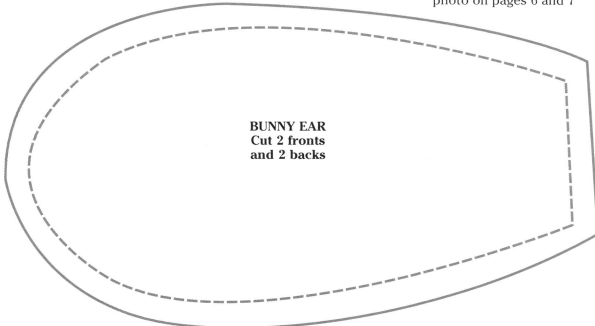

BUNNY EAR
**Cut 2 fronts
and 2 backs**

White Headband with Roses

FINISHED SIZE: 19" adjust to head measurement

FABRICS:
Mink-y Fleece:
⅛ yard White for headband
2" x 9" strip Lavender Mink-y
2" x 9" strip Pink Mink-y
3" x 15" Sage Green Mink-y

MATERIALS:
20" of 1" wide elastic
Needle and thread

CUTTING:
3" x 20" strip of White for the headband
2" x 9" strip Lavender for Rose
2" x 9" strip Pink for Rose
8 Sage leaves using pattern

INSTRUCTIONS:
All seam allowances are ¼".
Headband: Fold the headband in half lengthwise. Sew the long edge.
   Turn right side out.
   Insert elastic. Overlap the ends of the elastic.
   Sew across the elastic to secure.
   Fold raw ends of headband under and sew the edges together.
Roses: Fold rose strip lengthwise with wrong sides together.
   Sew the long edge with a gathering stitch.
   Lightly gather the strip.
   To form a rose, fold 1" of the end down to form a center. (See steps on page 15.)
   Hand stitch in place.
   Loosely wrap Mink-y around the center to form a flower.
   Hand sew and adjust fabric as you go.
   Tuck in the raw end.
   Stitch several times through the bottom of the rose to secure all layers.
Leaves: Place 2 leaves right sides together.
   Sew around the edges leaving the flat end open.
   Clip the curves. Turn right side out.
   Make 4 leaves.
Finishing: Hand stitch flowers and leaves onto headband.

Rose Headband

photo on page 15

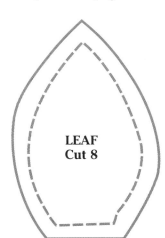

**LEAF
Cut 8**

After Bath Cuddle Wrap and Duck Toy

photo on page 10

After Bath Cuddle Wrap

FINISHED SIZE: 30" x 30"

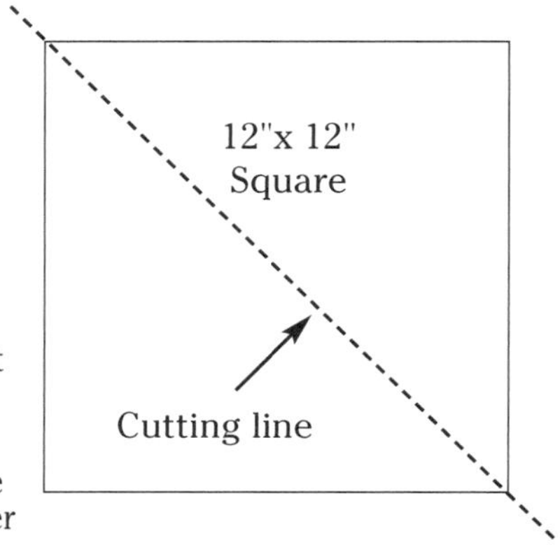

FABRICS:

Mink-y Fleece:
1 yard of Blue
¼ yard of Yellow for duck
1 yard of Blue print flannel
2" square of Orange polar fleece or felt
for duck beak

MATERIALS:

Sulky Yellow rayon thread for applique
Sulky self-adhesive Tear Away stabilizer
Black and Orange embroidery floss
Needle and thread

CUTTING:

31" x 31" flannel
31" x 31" Blue Mink-y
12" square of Mink-y and flannel cut on the diagonal for hood
1" x 14" strip Yellow Mink-y for duck hair
Yellow Mink-y duck head using pattern
Orange bill using pattern

INSTRUCTIONS:

All seam allowances are ¼".

Hood:

For loops at the top of the duck head, fold the Yellow Mink-y strip in thirds, lengthwise.
Zig-zag stitch down the center of the strip.
Place duck head on the center of the triangle.
Pin in place.
Adhere stabilizer to the flannel behind the head.

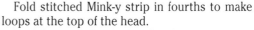

12"x 12"
Square

Cutting line

Fold stitched Mink-y strip in fourths to make loops at the top of the head.
Tuck loops under the head and pin in place.
Applique head, securing loops as you stitch.
Remove stabilizer. Embroider eyes with Black floss.
Pin the bill in place and stitch across the center. Embroider beak nostrils.
Place triangles right sides together. Stitch the long edge. Turn right side out.
Topstitch the long edge.

Blanket:

Pin hood to the corner of the blanket with Mink-y sides together.
Place flannel on top of blanket and hood, right sides together.
Pin layers together. Stitch layers together leaving a 5" opening for turning.
Clip corners.
Turn right side out. Hand stitch the opening closed.
Lightly press around edges. Pin and topstitch the edge.

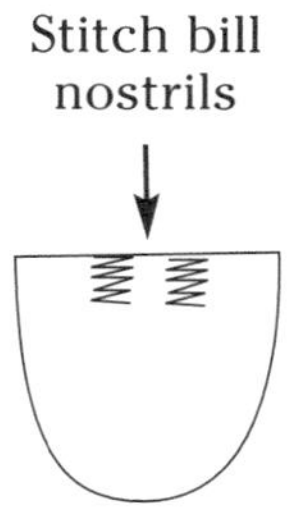

Stitch bill
nostrils

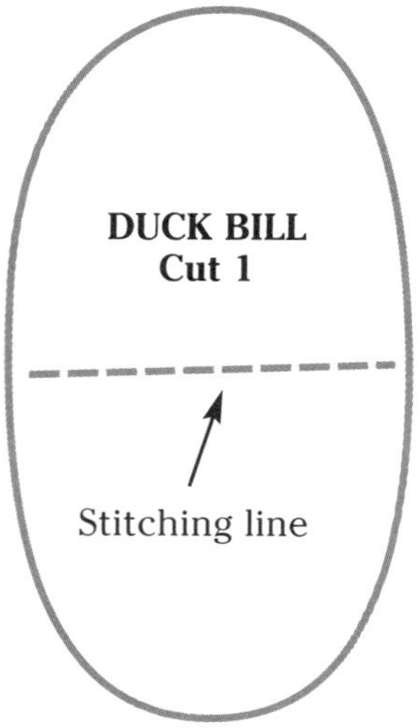

DUCK BILL
Cut 1

Stitching line

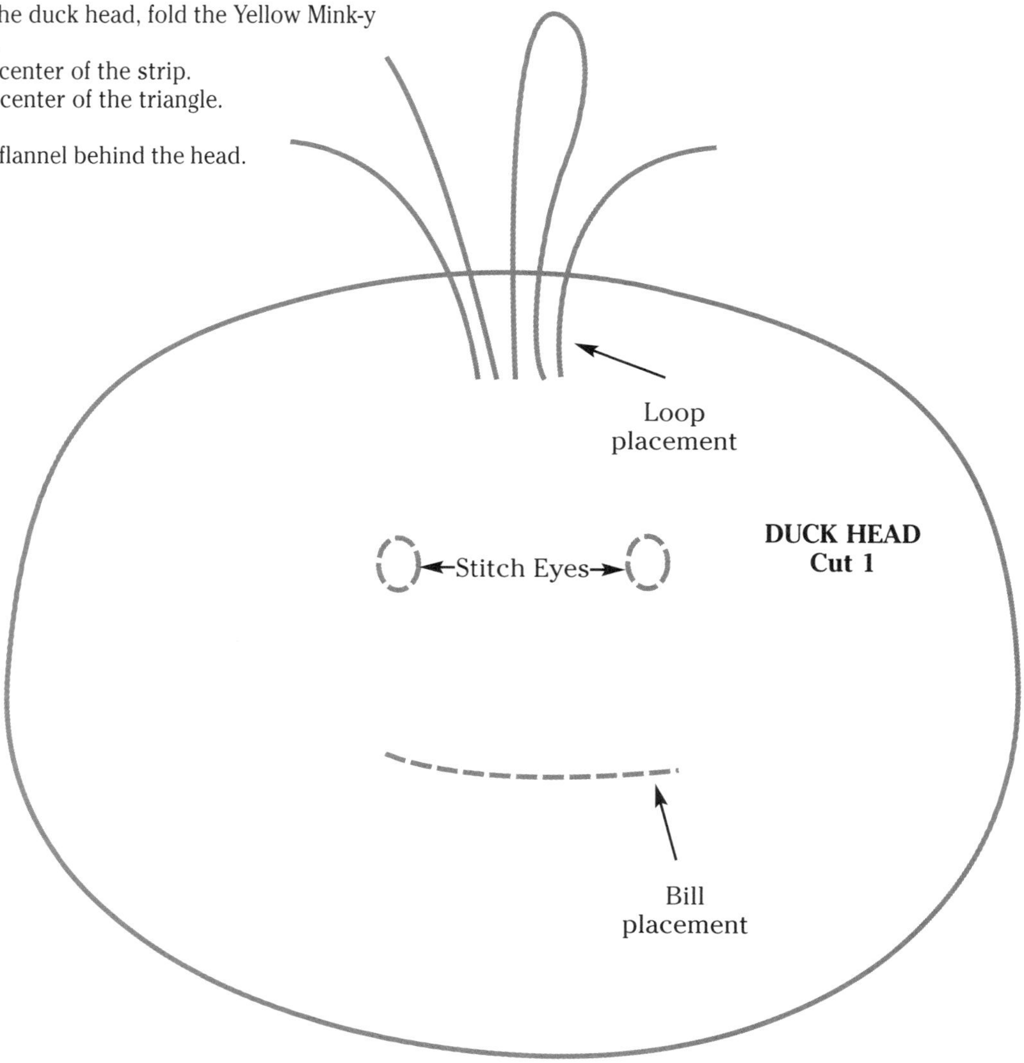

Loop
placement

←Stitch Eyes→

DUCK HEAD
Cut 1

Bill
placement

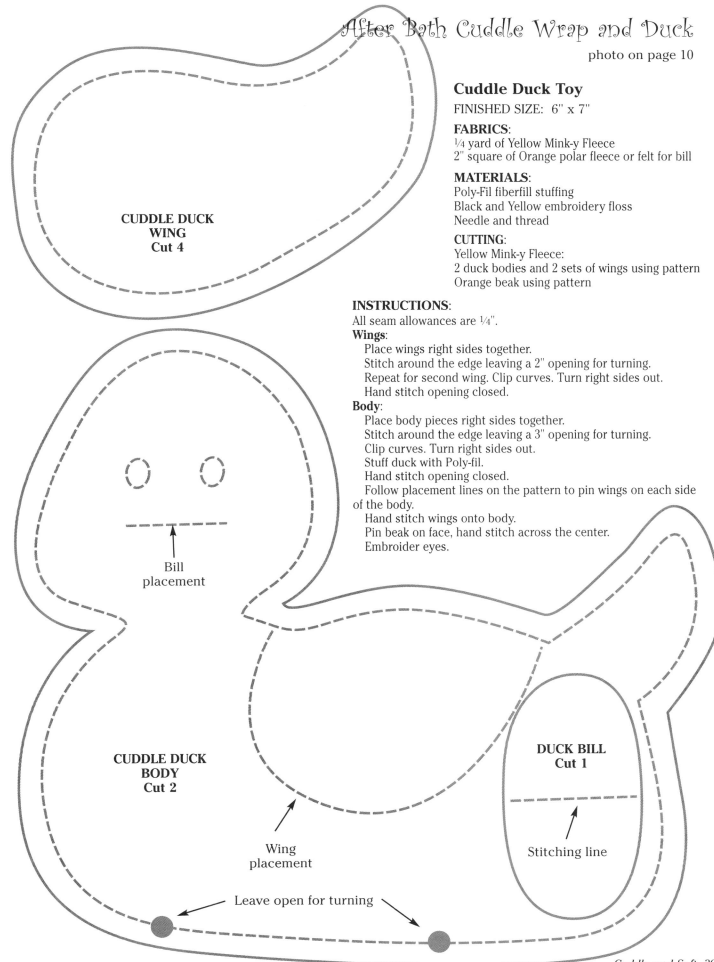

Cuddle Duck Toy

FINISHED SIZE: 6" x 7"

FABRICS:

¼ yard of Yellow Mink-y Fleece

2" square of Orange polar fleece or felt for bill

MATERIALS:

Poly-Fil fiberfill stuffing

Black and Yellow embroidery floss

Needle and thread

CUTTING:

Yellow Mink-y Fleece:

2 duck bodies and 2 sets of wings using pattern

Orange beak using pattern

INSTRUCTIONS:

All seam allowances are ¼".

Wings:

Place wings right sides together.

Stitch around the edge leaving a 2" opening for turning.

Repeat for second wing. Clip curves. Turn right sides out.

Hand stitch opening closed.

Body:

Place body pieces right sides together.

Stitch around the edge leaving a 3" opening for turning.

Clip curves. Turn right sides out.

Stuff duck with Poly-fil.

Hand stitch opening closed.

Follow placement lines on the pattern to pin wings on each side of the body.

Hand stitch wings onto body.

Pin beak on face, hand stitch across the center.

Embroider eyes.

CUDDLE DUCK
WING
Cut 4

CUDDLE DUCK
BODY
Cut 2

Bill
placement

Wing
placement

DUCK BILL
Cut 1

Stitching line

Leave open for turning

Mink-y Pals

photo on page 11

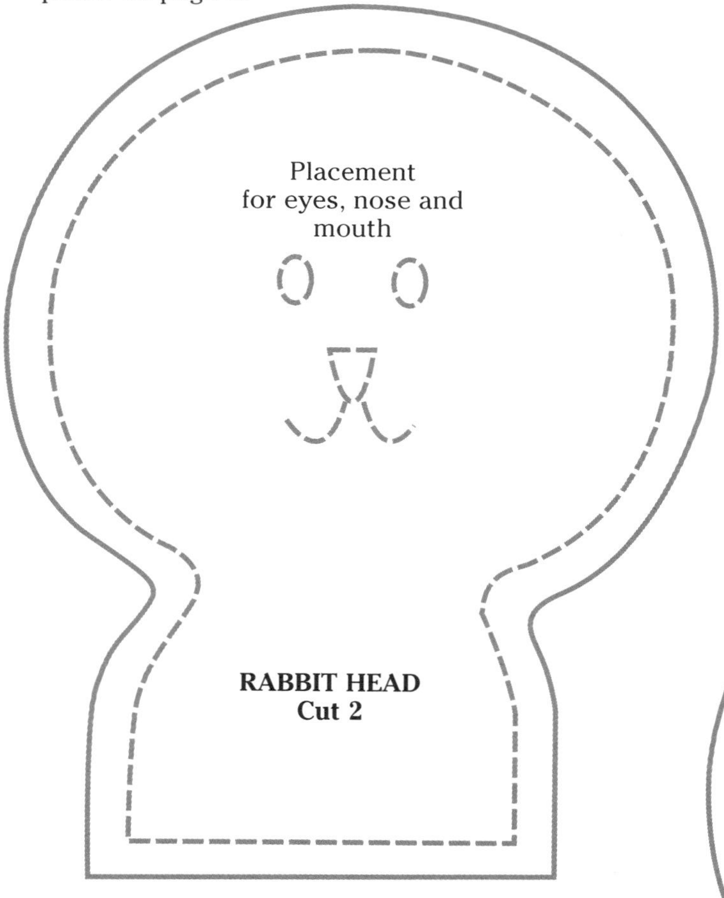

Placement
for eyes, nose and
mouth

RABBIT HEAD
Cut 2

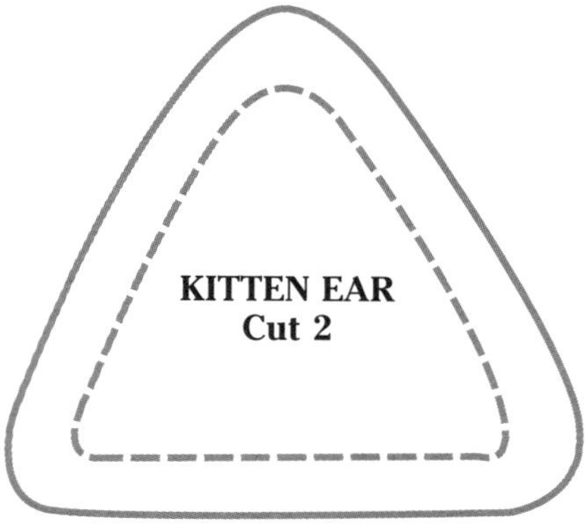

KITTEN EAR
Cut 2

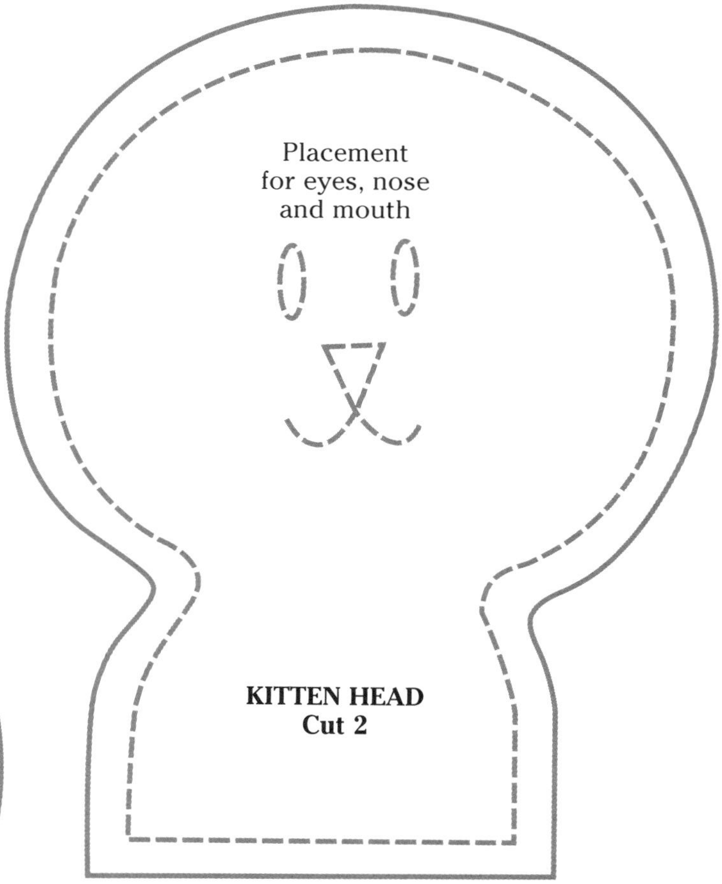

Placement
for eyes, nose
and mouth

KITTEN HEAD
Cut 2

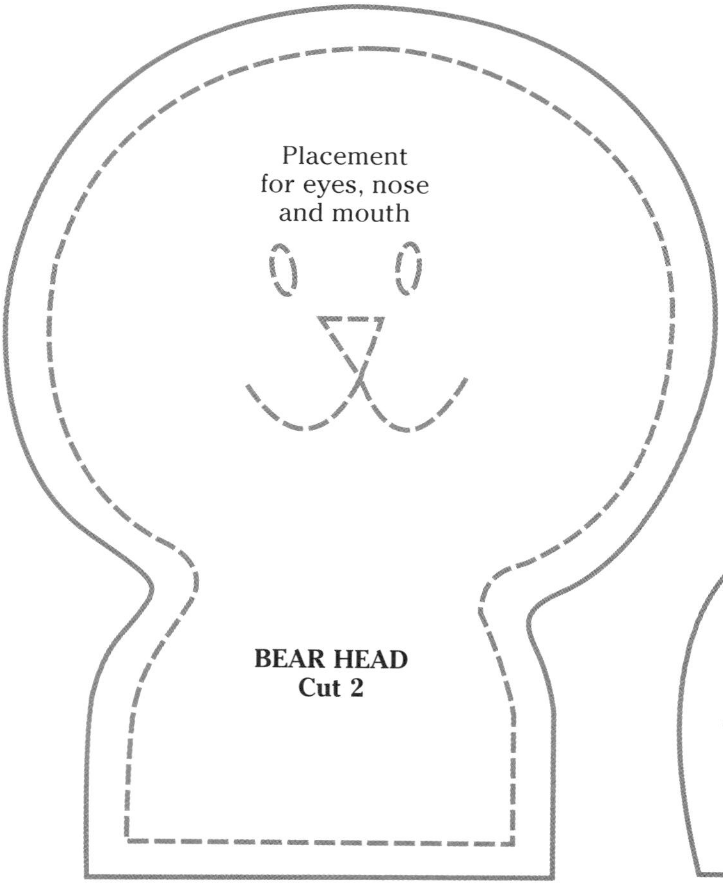

Placement
for eyes, nose
and mouth

BEAR HEAD
Cut 2

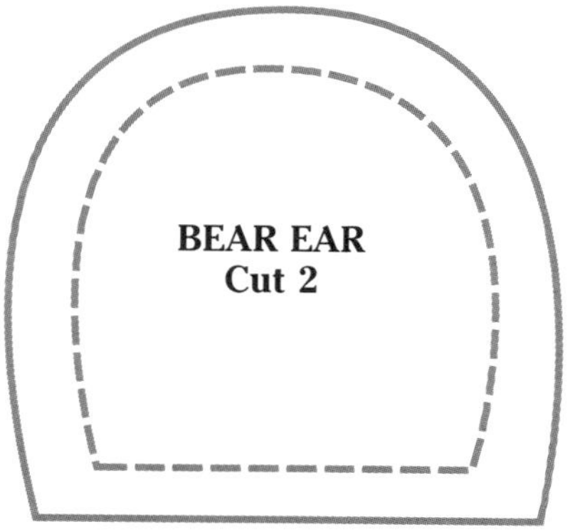

BEAR EAR
Cut 2

FINISHED SIZE: 4" x 14"

FABRICS:

Mink-y Fleece:

½ yard desired color for body

6" x 6" contrasting color for collar

8" x 10" desired color for animal head

MATERIALS:

Poly-Fil stuffing

12" ribbon for bow

Black and Pink embroidery floss for faces

Needle and thread

CUTTING:

4 Mink-y ear pieces using pattern

2 heads using pattern

1 Mink-y 14" square for body

1 contrasting Mink-y 6" square for collar

INSTRUCTIONS:

All seam allowances are ¼".

Head:

Pin right sides of ears together.

Sew around edge, leaving the bottom open for turning.

Clip curves. Turn right side out.

Repeat for second ear.

Pin ears to the top edge of the head, matching raw edges.

Pin head pieces right sides together.

Sew around, leaving the bottom open for turning.

Clip curves. Turn right side out.

Firmly stuff and hand stitch the opening closed.

Embroider the face using 2 strands of embroidery floss.

For duck, hand stitch bill to face.

Body:

Diagonally fold each square into 4ths. (See photo on page 11.)

Cut ½" from folded inside corner to make a hole in the middle.

Finishing:

Place body right side up on table.

Place contrast collar right side up on top of body.

Align holes in center of both pieces.

Insert neck through body and collar pieces.

Hand stitch through both layers and through neck to secure.

Tie a ribbon bow around the neck.

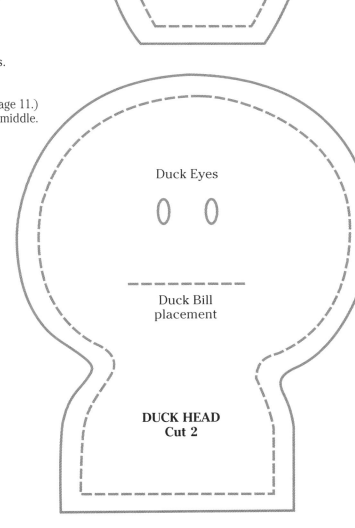

RABBIT EAR
Cut 2

Duck Eyes

0 0

Duck Bill
placement

Stitching
line

DUCK BILL Cut 1

DUCK HEAD Cut 2

So Soft Bean Bag Teddy

photo on page 3

Ear Placement

Stitch Face

**BEAR BODY
Cut 2**

**BEAR
EAR
Cut 4**

Body:
   With right sides together, pin the bear front to the back.
   Stitch all around, leaving a 3" opening at the side of a leg for turning.
   Clip curves.
   Turn right side out.
   Stuff the bear with pellets.
   Hand stitch the opening closed.

Face:
   Use floss to embroider face.
   To start, make the knot in the middle of the eye or nose and cover it with Satin stitch.
   Use a Backstitch to embroider the mouth.

Bow tie:
   Fold the 2½" x 6" tie in half lengthwise right sides together.
   Stitch long end. Turn right side out.
   Fold the ends to the center and stitch in place.
   Fold the 1" square into thirds, right sides out.
   Wrap it around the center of the tie to hide the stitching.
   Stitch the ends together in back of the tie.
   Stitch bow tie to neck of bear.

Teddy Bear

FINISHED SIZE: 11"

FABRICS:
Mink-y Fleece:
   ⅓ yard Honey Brown
   3" x 8" Red

MATERIALS:
Stuffing pellets
Black embroidery floss
Needle and thread

CUTTING:
4 ears and 2 bodies from
   Honey Brown
2½" x 6" and 1" square
   for bow tie from Red

INSTRUCTIONS:
All seam allowances
are ¼".

Ears:
   Place 2 ear pieces right sides together.
   Stitch the edges leaving the bottom open for turning.
   Clip curves. Turn right side out.
   Repeat for second ear.
   Pin ears to the head matching raw edges.
   Baste in place.

Leave open
for turning

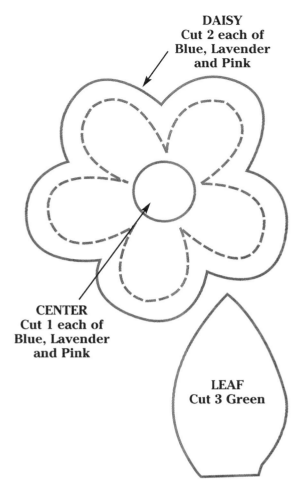

DAISY
Cut 2 each of
Blue, Lavender
and Pink

CENTER
Cut 1 each of
Blue, Lavender
and Pink

LEAF
Cut 3 Green

Pink Daisy Headband

FINISHED SIZE: 19" adjust to head measure

FABRICS:

Mink-y Fleece:
   1/8 yard Pink for headband and flower
   4" x 8" Light Blue
   4" x 8" Lavender
   One 3" square Sage Green

MATERIALS:

20" of 1" wide elastic
Needle and thread

CUTTING:

3" x 20" strip of Pink for the headband
2 Pink, 2 Blue, and 2 Lavender flowers using pattern
6 Sage leaves using pattern
1 flower center from Pink, Blue, and Lavender using pattern

INSTRUCTIONS:

All seam allowances are 1/4".

Headband:

   Fold headband in half lengthwise. Sew the long edge.
   Turn right side out.
   Insert elastic. Overlap the ends of the elastic.
   Sew across the elastic to secure.
   Fold raw ends of headband under and sew the edges together.

Flowers:

   With right sides together, sew around all edges.
   Clip curves. Make a 1/2" slit in the center of each flower.
   Turn right side out.
   Pin flower center to the middle of the daisy.
   Applique around the edge.

Leaves:

   Place 2 leaves right sides together.
   Sew around the edges leaving the flat end open.
   Clip the curves. Turn right side out.
   Make 3 leaves.

Finishing: Hand stitch flowers and leaves onto headband.

Heart Burp Cloth

FINISHED SIZE: 11" x 19"

FABRICS:

1/8 yard Pink or Blue Dot Mink-y Fleece
1/4 yard flannel
4" x 5" scrap of Pink chenille for heart applique

MATERIALS:

Sulky self-adhesive Tear Away stabilizer
Needle and thread

CUTTING:

Four 3" x 20" strips of Mink-y
Two 7" x 20" strips of flannel
1 Pink chenille heart from pattern

INSTRUCTIONS:

All seam allowances are 1/4".
Sew a Mink-y strip to both sides of each piece of flannel.
Press seams open. Pin heart in place.
Adhere stabilizer to the Mink-y behind heart.
Applique the heart in place.
With right sides together, pin the front to the back.
Sew all the way around, leaving a 3" opening for turning.
Turn right side out.
Hand stitch the opening closed.
Topstitch all the way around the edge.

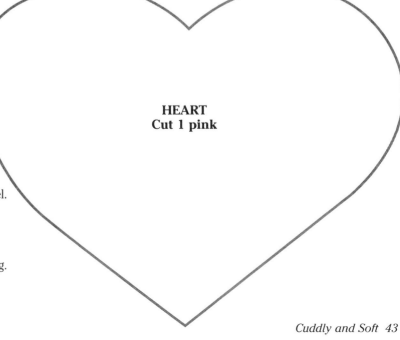

HEART
Cut 1 pink

Ziggy Zaggy Car Quilt

photo on page 13

Ziggy Zaggy Car Quilt

FINISHED SIZE: 27" x 36"

FABRICS:

Mink-y Fleece:

½ yard of Red Dot

1 yard of Green Dot for back

½ yard of Blue car print flannel

MATERIALS:

Red embroidery floss for tying

Needle and thread

CUTTING:

12 full size blocks each of Red Dot and Blue flannel

3 left half blocks each of Red Dot and Blue flannel

3 right half blocks each of Red Dot and Blue flannel

27½" x 36½" Green Dot for backing

INSTRUCTIONS:

All seam allowances are ¼".

Assembly:

Follow the Assembly Diagram to make 6 rows.

Three rows start with Red. Three rows start with Blue flannel.

Sew the rows together. Press seam allowances open.

Backing:

Place the backing on the pieced top with right sides together.

Pin all layers.

Stitch around the perimeter, leaving an 8" opening for turning.

Clip the corners. Turn right side out. Gently press edges. Topstitch ¼" all around the edge.

Finishing:

Using 6 strands of floss, tie the quilt as indicated on the Assembly Diagram or as desired.

From top of blankee, insert needle through both layers leaving a 4" tail of floss on top of blankee.

Insert needle into back of blankee, draw needle and floss through to top.

Tie the floss in a double knot to secure the layers.

Trim floss ends to ½".

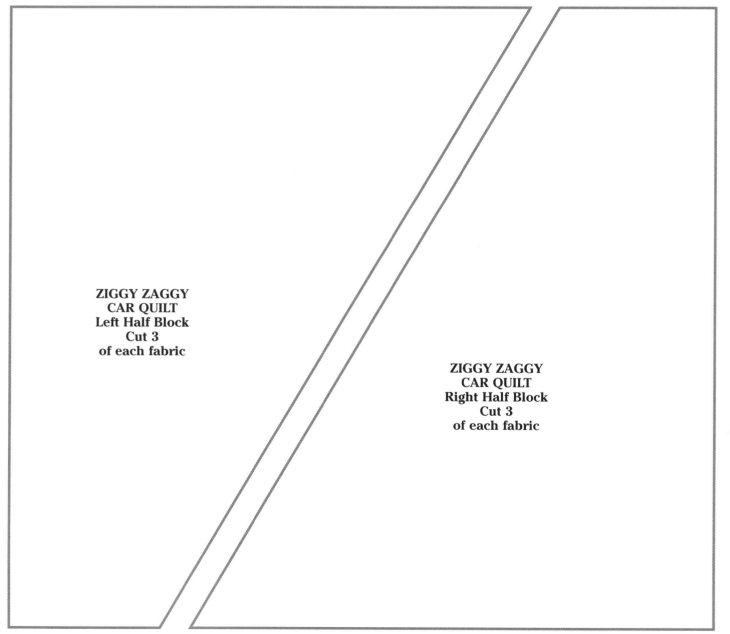

ZIGGY ZAGGY
CAR QUILT
Left Half Block
Cut 3
of each fabric

ZIGGY ZAGGY
CAR QUILT
Right Half Block
Cut 3
of each fabric

Assembly Diagram

● = tying

**ZIGGY ZAGGY
CAR QUILT
Full Block
Cut 12
of each fabric**

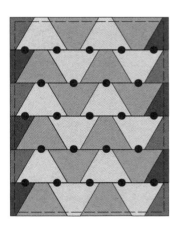

Assembly Diagram

Mink-y Motor Car Pillow Toys

photo on page 13

instructions on page 48

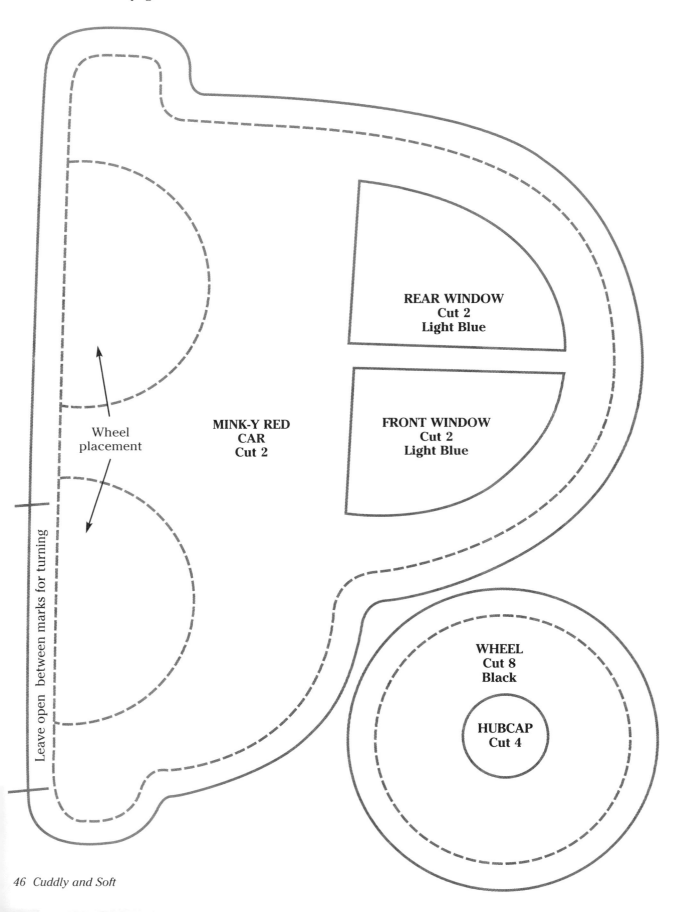

REAR WINDOW
Cut 2
Light Blue

FRONT WINDOW
Cut 2
Light Blue

MINK-Y RED
CAR
Cut 2

Wheel
placement

Leave open between marks for turning

WHEEL
Cut 8
Black

HUBCAP
Cut 4

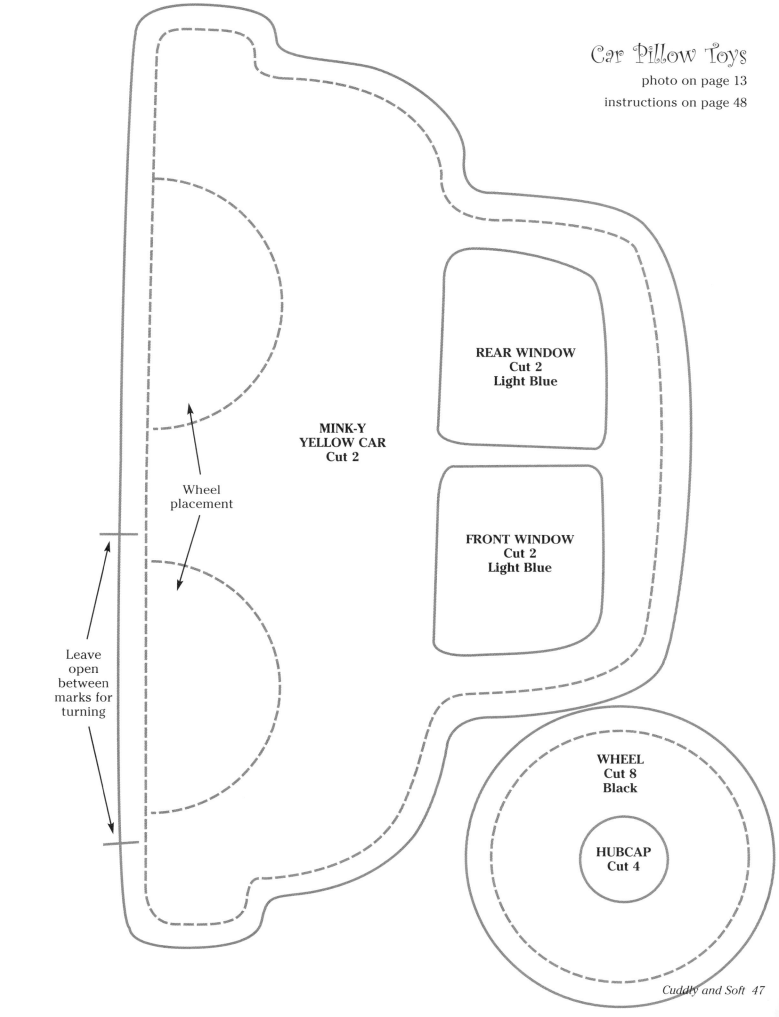

Car Pillow Toys

photo on page 13

instructions on page 48

REAR WINDOW
Cut 2
Light Blue

MINK-Y
YELLOW CAR
Cut 2

Wheel
placement

FRONT WINDOW
Cut 2
Light Blue

Leave
open
between
marks for
turning

WHEEL
Cut 8
Black

HUBCAP
Cut 4

Cuddly and Soft 47

Mink-y Motor Car Pillow Toys

photo on page 13

patterns on pages 46 - 47

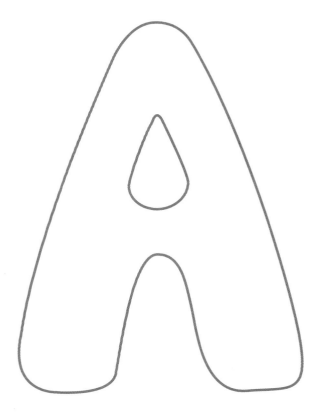

FINISHED SIZE: Yellow Car 6" x 10", Red Car 6" x 8"

FABRICS:
Mink-y Fleece:
   ¼ yard desired color for car body
   ⅛ yard Light Blue for windows
   ⅛ yard Black for tires
   2" x 4" desired color for hubcaps

MATERIALS:
Poly-Fil stuffing
Sulky self-adhesive Tear Away stabilizer
Sulky rayon thread for applique (Light Blue, Yellow, Red)
Needle and thread

INSTRUCTIONS:
All seam allowances are ¼".
Cutting: Place car color Mink-y right sides together.
   Pin pattern to Mink-y. Cut 2 car pieces from Mink-y.
   From Light Blue Mink-y, cut 2 front windows and 2 back windows.
   From Black Mink-y, cut 8 tires.
   Cut 4 hubcaps from colored Mink-y scraps.
Applique: Place window right side up on the right side of Mink-y.
   See pattern for placement.
   Adhere stabilizer on back of car Mink-y behind window.
   Applique window.
   Repeat for remaining 3 windows.
   Tear away excess stabilizer.
Assembly: Pin car pieces right sides together.
   Sew together leaving an opening for turning.
   Clip curves. Turn right side out.
   Stuff. Hand stitch opening closed.
Tires: Place 2 tire pieces right sides together.
   Sew together all around the edge. Clip curves.
   Make a small slit through the center of one layer of the tire.
   Turn right side out.
   Place a hubcap piece in the center of the tire over the slit.
   Applique in place.
   Repeat for 3 more tires.
   See photo for tire placement. Hand stitch tires to car.

Mink-y Cube

FINISHED SIZE: 6"

FABRICS:
6" x 10" piece of 6 different colors of Mink-y Fleece

MATERIALS:
Poly-Fil fiberfill stuffing
Sulky rayon thread for applique
Sulky self-adhesive Tear Away stabilizer
Needle and thread

CUTTING:
One 6" square from each color Mink-y
Letters and numbers

INSTRUCTIONS:
All seam allowances are ¼".
Applique:
   Pin a number or letter right side up on the right side of Mink-y square.
   Adhere stabilizer to back of square.
   Applique using rayon thread.
   Repeat for all 6 squares. Tear away excess stabilizer.
Assembly:
   Pin 2 squares with right sides together.
   Beginning ¼" from the corner, sew a seam, stopping ¼" from the end.
   Continue sewing squares together in the same manner to form a cube.
   Leave a 4" opening on the last seam for turning.
   Clip corners. Turn right side out.
Finish:
   Stuff with Poly-fil stuffing. Hand stitch the opening closed.

Jewel Tone Quilt

photo on page 14

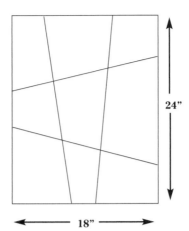

24"

18"

Cutting diagram A

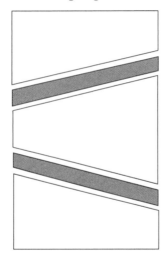

Cutting diagram B
and Strip Piecing Diagram

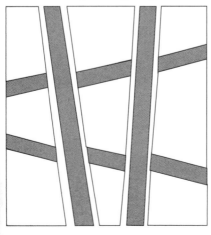

FINISHED SIZE: 31" x 37"

FABRICS:

Mink-y Fleece:
½ yard Dark Green
½ yard Purple Dot
1 yard of Blue print flannel
¼ yard each of 6-8 different flannel prints

MATERIALS:

Needle and thread

INSTRUCTIONS:

All seam allowances are ¼".

Pieced flannel:

Cut 12 flannel rectangles 6" x 10".

Cut those pieces into wedge shapes of varying sizes.

Use pattern if desired, or cut randomly without a pattern.

Place 2 wedges right sides together. Sew the long edge.

Continue adding wedges, alternating the wide and narrow ends.

Press all seams in one direction. Cut the strip lengthwise into 2 long strips measuring 2½" wide.

Piecing top:

Cut Purple Dot 18" x 24".

Cut into 3 sections following Cutting diagram A.

Assembly Diagram:

Sew the strips together with a pieced flannel strip in between.

Gently press seams open.

Cut into 3 sections as shown in Cutting diagram B.

Sew the strips together with a pieced flannel strip in between. Gently press seams open.

Trim edges to square top up to 19½" x 26".

Border:

From Green Mink-y, cut a top and bottom border 6" x 19½".

Stitch border piece to each end of pieced top. Press seams open.

Cut 2 side borders 6" x 36½". Stitch border piece to each side of pieced top.

Backing:

From flannel, cut one piece measuring 30½" x 36½".

Place flannel wrong side up on table.

Place pieced top right side up on top.

Binding:

From flannel, cut 3 strips measuring 2" x 38".

Sew ends together at angles to make one strip 140" long.

Press one end under ½".

Fold in half lengthwise, wrong sides together.

Press. Pin raw edge of binding to raw edges of blankee.

Pin all around. Tuck raw end into folded end. Trim excess.

Sew through all layers. Clip corners.

Fold binding towards back of quilt.

Hand stitch in place.

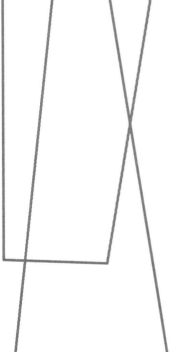

WEDGE PATTERN

NOTE: Wedge patterns are approximate and may vary from wedge strip to wedge strip.

WEDGE PATTERN

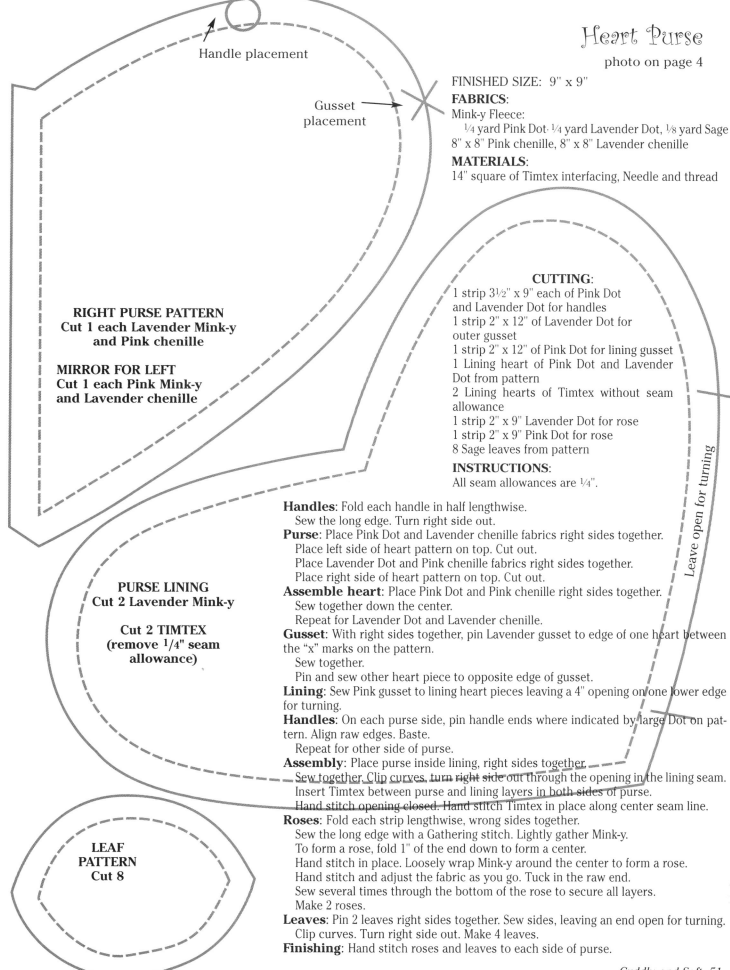

Handle placement

Gusset
placement

FINISHED SIZE: 9" x 9"

FABRICS:
Mink-y Fleece:
¼ yard Pink Dot. ¼ yard Lavender Dot, ⅛ yard Sage
8" x 8" Pink chenille, 8" x 8" Lavender chenille

MATERIALS:
14" square of Timtex interfacing, Needle and thread

RIGHT PURSE PATTERN
Cut 1 each Lavender Mink-y
and Pink chenille

MIRROR FOR LEFT
Cut 1 each Pink Mink-y
and Lavender chenille

CUTTING:
1 strip 3½" x 9" each of Pink Dot
and Lavender Dot for handles
1 strip 2" x 12" of Lavender Dot for
outer gusset
1 strip 2" x 12" of Pink Dot for lining gusset
1 Lining heart of Pink Dot and Lavender
Dot from pattern
2 Lining hearts of Timtex without seam
allowance
1 strip 2" x 9" Lavender Dot for rose
1 strip 2" x 9" Pink Dot for rose
8 Sage leaves from pattern

INSTRUCTIONS:
All seam allowances are ¼".

Leave open for turning

PURSE LINING
Cut 2 Lavender Mink-y

Cut 2 TIMTEX
(remove ¼" seam
allowance)

Handles: Fold each handle in half lengthwise.
Sew the long edge. Turn right side out.
Purse: Place Pink Dot and Lavender chenille fabrics right sides together.
Place left side of heart pattern on top. Cut out.
Place Lavender Dot and Pink chenille fabrics right sides together.
Place right side of heart pattern on top. Cut out.
Assemble heart: Place Pink Dot and Pink chenille right sides together.
Sew together down the center.
Repeat for Lavender Dot and Lavender chenille.
Gusset: With right sides together, pin Lavender gusset to edge of one heart between
the "x" marks on the pattern.
Sew together.
Pin and sew other heart piece to opposite edge of gusset.
Lining: Sew Pink gusset to lining heart pieces leaving a 4" opening on one lower edge
for turning.
Handles: On each purse side, pin handle ends where indicated by large Dot on pat-
tern. Align raw edges. Baste.
Repeat for other side of purse.
Assembly: Place purse inside lining, right sides together.
Sew together. Clip curves, turn right side out through the opening in the lining seam.
Insert Timtex between purse and lining layers in both sides of purse.
Hand stitch opening closed. Hand stitch Timtex in place along center seam line.
Roses: Fold each strip lengthwise, wrong sides together.
Sew the long edge with a Gathering stitch. Lightly gather Mink-y.
To form a rose, fold 1" of the end down to form a center.
Hand stitch in place. Loosely wrap Mink-y around the center to form a rose.
Hand stitch and adjust the fabric as you go. Tuck in the raw end.
Sew several times through the bottom of the rose to secure all layers.
Make 2 roses.
Leaves: Pin 2 leaves right sides together. Sew sides, leaving an end open for turning.
Clip curves. Turn right side out. Make 4 leaves.
Finishing: Hand stitch roses and leaves to each side of purse.

**LEAF
PATTERN
Cut 8**

Kitty Poncho and Doll

photo on page 15

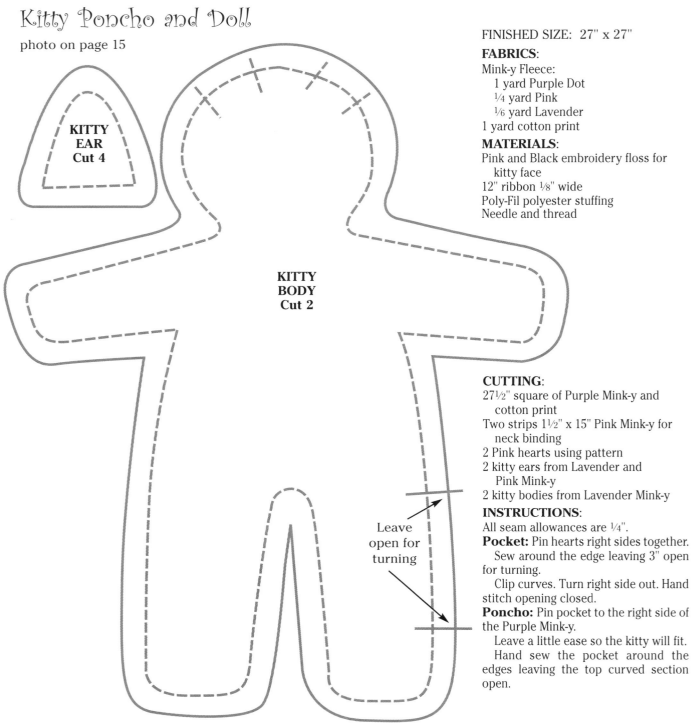

KITTY EAR Cut 4

KITTY BODY Cut 2

Leave open for turning

FINISHED SIZE: 27" x 27"

FABRICS:
Mink-y Fleece:
   1 yard Purple Dot
   ¼ yard Pink
   ⅙ yard Lavender
1 yard cotton print

MATERIALS:
Pink and Black embroidery floss for kitty face
12" ribbon ⅛" wide
Poly-Fil polyester stuffing
Needle and thread

CUTTING:
27½" square of Purple Mink-y and cotton print
Two strips 1½" x 15" Pink Mink-y for neck binding
2 Pink hearts using pattern
2 kitty ears from Lavender and Pink Mink-y
2 kitty bodies from Lavender Mink-y

INSTRUCTIONS:
All seam allowances are ¼".

Pocket: Pin hearts right sides together. Sew around the edge leaving 3" open for turning.
   Clip curves. Turn right side out. Hand stitch opening closed.

Poncho: Pin pocket to the right side of the Purple Mink-y.
   Leave a little ease so the kitty will fit.
   Hand sew the pocket around the edges leaving the top curved section open.

Assembly:
Pin Mink-y and cotton poncho pieces right sides together.
Sew all around, leaving a 6" opening for turning.
Clip corners. Turn right side out. Gently press the edges.
Hand stitch opening closed.
Topstitch all around ¼" from edge.
Use the pattern to mark the neck opening.
Cut through both layers of the poncho.

Finishing:
Fold one short end of each binding strip down ½".
Begin at the inside end of the slit and pin strip to both raw edges of neck hole.
Pin all around neck to end of opposite slit. Fold under end. Sew in place.
Repeat for other side of neck.

Fold neck binding to inside of poncho.
Fold under ¼" of raw edge. Hand stitch to secure.

Pocket Kitty:
Pin 2 ear pieces right sides together.
Stitch together, leaving the bottom edge open for turning.
Clip curves. Turn right side out.
Place right side of ears to right sides of Mink-y at top of head matching raw edges. Baste.
Pin both body pieces right sides together.
Stitch all around, leaving a 2" opening for turning. Clip curves. Turn right side out.
Lightly stuff kitty. Hand stitch opening closed.
Use floss to embroider face. Tie ribbon bow around neck.
Tuck into pocket of poncho.

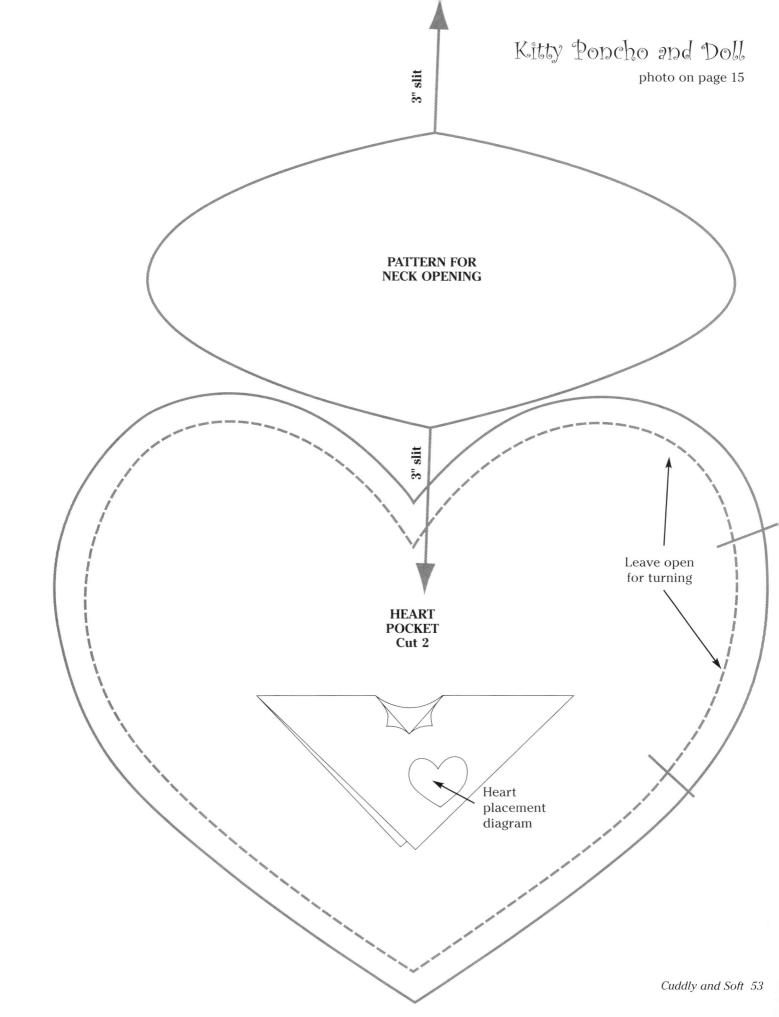

3" slit

**PATTERN FOR
NECK OPENING**

3" slit

Leave open
for turning

**HEART
POCKET
Cut 2**

Heart
placement
diagram

Three Bears

photo on page 16

Chenille Bear

FINISHED SIZE: 11"

FABRICS:
⅓ yard Chenille

MATERIALS:
Poly-Fil polyester stuffing
Black embroidery floss
12" ribbon
Needle and thread

CUTTING:
4 ears and 2 bodies

INSTRUCTIONS:
All seam allowances are ¼".
Ears: Place 2 ear pieces right sides together.
   Stitch the edges leaving the bottom open for turning.
   Clip curves.
   Turn right side out.
   Repeat for second ear.
   Pin ears to head matching raw edges.
   Baste in place.
Body: With right sides together, pin the bear front to the back.
   Stitch all around, leaving a 3" opening at the side of a leg for turning.
   Clip curves.
   Turn right side out.
   Stuff the bear.
   Hand stitch the opening closed.
Finish: Use floss to embroider face.
   Make the knot in the middle of the eye or nose and cover it with Satin stitch.
   Use a Backstitch to embroider the mouth.
   Tie a ribbon around the neck.

Ear Placement

Stitch Face

BEAR
EAR
Cut 4

BEAR
BODY
Cut 2

Leave open
for turning

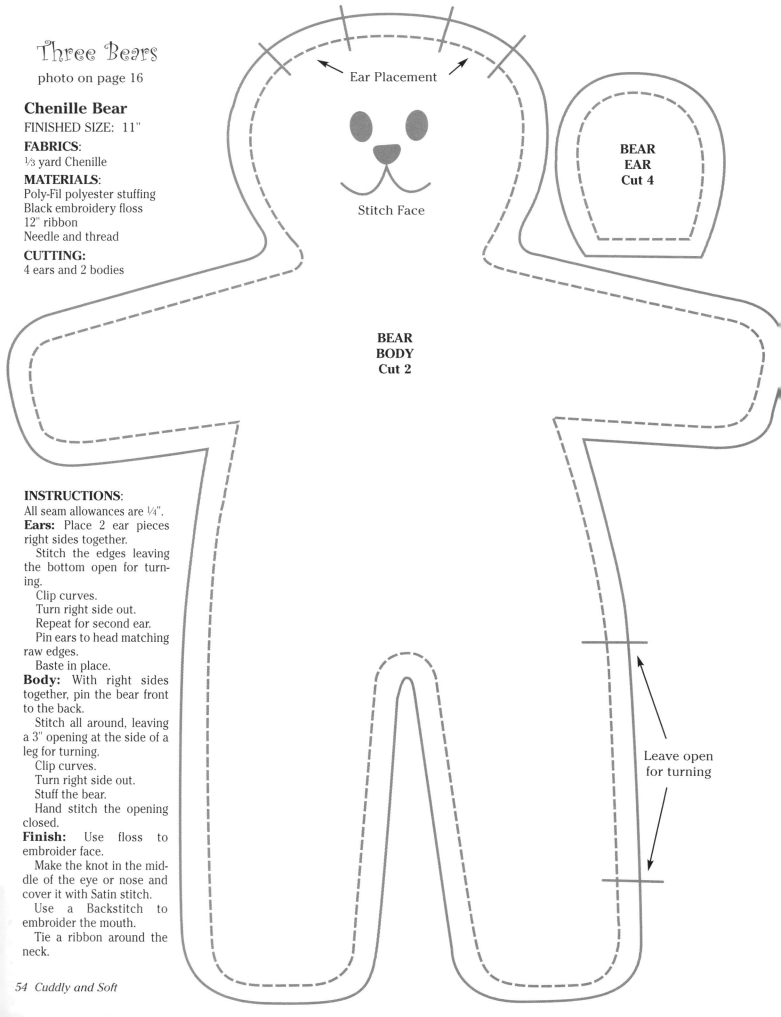

Puffed Flowers Blankee

FINISHED SIZE: 26" x 35"

FABRICS:

Mink-y Fleece:
- ¼ yard of Yellow
- ¼ yard of Pink

¼ yard of 3 different Floral flannels
¼ yard of Yellow chenille
1 yard of Pink chenille for the back

MATERIALS:

Sulky Yellow rayon thread for applique
Light Pink embroidery floss
Needle and thread

CUTTING:

Thirty-four 3½" squares of assorted flannel for sashing
Thirty-eight 1½" x 3½" of assorted flannel for border
Four 1½" squares of flannel for the corners
Six 6½" x 9½" of Yellow Mink-y
Three 6½" x 9½" of Yellow chenille
One 27" x 36" Pink chenille for the back
Nine flowers with 2 layers of Pink Mink-y (See pattern)
Nine flower centers from Yellow Mink-y (See pattern)

INSTRUCTIONS:

All seam allowances are ¼".

Sashing: Sew the flannel squares together to make 6 rows of 3 squares and 2 rows of 8 squares. Sew a 1½" x 3½" rectangle to both ends of the 8-square strips.

Border: Sew the flannel rectangles together to make 6 rows of 1½" x 9½" for the side borders. Set aside.

Sew the flannel rectangles together to make 2 rows 1½" x 24½".

Sew a 1½" square to each end of these two rows for the top and bottom borders.

Assembling top: See the Assembly diagram.

Rows 1 & 3: Side border, Mink-y, Sashing, Mink-y, Sashing, Chenille, Side border.

Row 2: Side border, Chenille, Sashing, Mink-y, Sashing, Mink-y, Side border.

Press seams open to avoid bulk.

Sew the rows together, adding long sashing strips between rows. Press the seams open.

Backing: Place Quilt on Chenille backing with right sides together.

Pin securely along all sides.

Stitch around all sides, leaving a 6" opening to turn.

Clip corners; turn right side out. Hand stitch opening closed.Press the edges.

Topstitch ¼" from the edge.

Quilting: Tie the quilt layers together with 3 strands of embroidery floss.

From top, insert needle into blankee, pull floss through, leaving a 3" tail on top.

Insert needle into back of blankee, pull needle and floss through to top.

Tie floss in a Surgeon's knot (see page 64). Trim ends as desired.

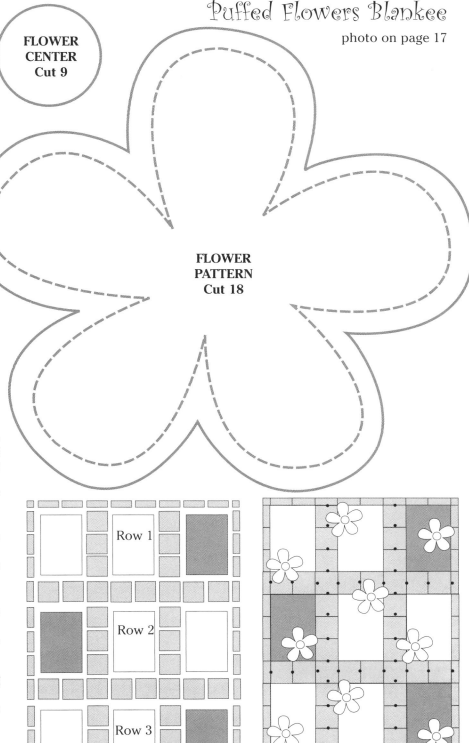

FLOWER CENTER Cut 9

FLOWER PATTERN Cut 18

Row 1

Row 2

Row 3

Assembly diagram
(• = ties on quilt)

Flowers: Place Mink-y right sides together and cut out each flower.

Pin layers together. Sew all around the flower. Clip curves.

Make small snip through one layer in the center of flowers; turn right sides out.

Pin the Yellow center in place.

Applique all around through all layers.

Place flowers on blankee.

Hand stitch a line from the center to the middle of each petal through all layers.

Cowboy Quilt

photo on page 12

Right side of fabric

Wrong side of fabric

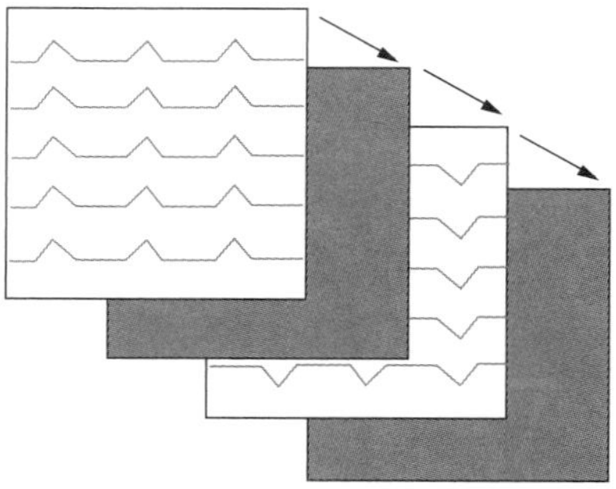

1. Stack four fabric squares together, alternating fabrics (2 sets with right sides together). The patterned fabric represents the cowboy print, the plain the Mink-y

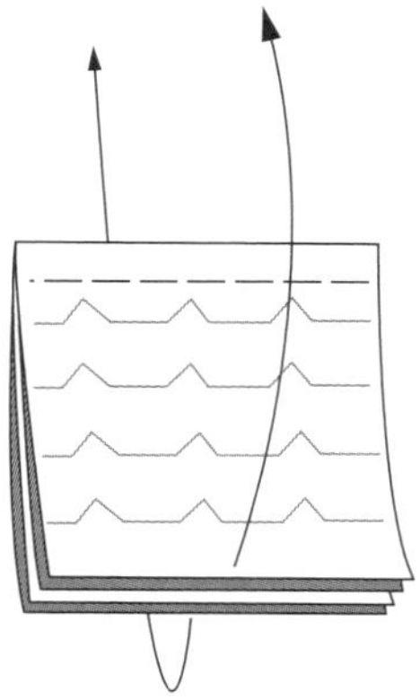

2. Stitch across top, turn top and bottom layers up.

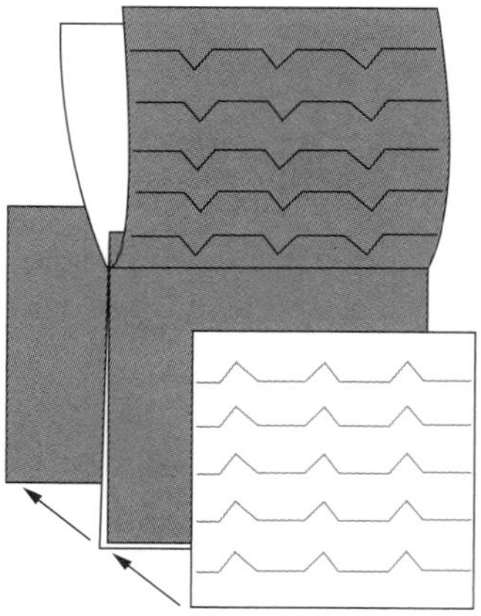

3. Stack two new layers on top and below bottom two layers and sew across bottom edge.

Cozy Cowboy Blankee

FINISHED SIZE: 24" x 31"

FABRICS:

Mink-y Fleece

½ yard of Red Dot

¼ yard of Gold Dot

10" x 12" Light Brown for horse applique

4" x 8" Dark Brown for boots and saddle applique

½ yard each of 2 cotton Cowboy prints

MATERIALS:

Sulky self-adhesive Tear Away stabilizer

Sulky rayon thread for applique (Yellow, Brown, Light Brown)

Dark Brown embroidery floss

Needle and thread

CUTTING:

Seven 4½" x 21½" strips from each Red Dot and print cotton

6 Gold stars using pattern

2 Dark Brown boots (one with toe pointing left, one with toe pointing right)

2 Light Brown horses (one facing left, one facing right) using pattern

2 Dark Brown saddles using pattern

Gold Borders:

2 sides 3½" x 28½"

Top and bottom 3½" x 24½"

INSTRUCTIONS:

All seam allowances are ¼".

Applique:

See photo for placement.

Pin horses and boots in place on Red Dot strips.

Adhere stabilizer to back of fabric behind the applique motif.

Using rayon thread, applique motif onto Mink-y.

Tear away excess stabilizer.

Repeat for all horse and boot appliques.

Applique saddle piece on back of horses.

Use Brown embroidery floss to embroider face and mane.

Lightly press from wrong side.

Assembly:

You are going to be stacking 4 layers, sewing a seam, and unfolding.

This technique allows you to form the front and back of the quilt with all seams inside.

Since the Red Mink-y has an applique, it has a top/bottom orientation.

Pay attention to the direction of the Mink-y as you stack so the images end up right side up on the quilt.

If your Cowboy fabric has a one-way design, pay attention to the orientation.

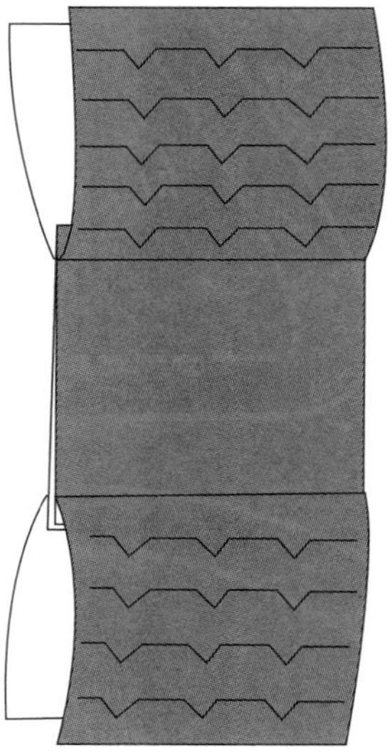

4. Turn down top and bottom layers.

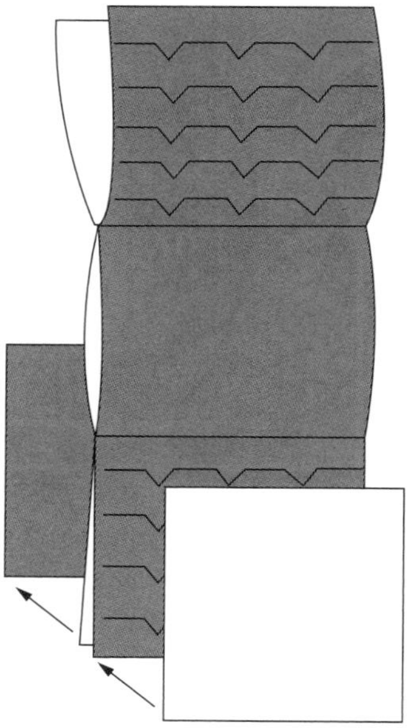

5. Stack two more layers on top and bottom of bottom layers and sew across bottom edge.

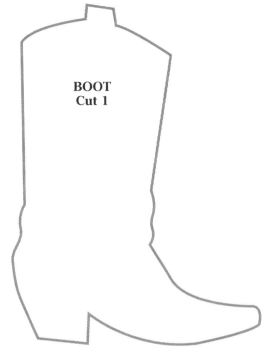

**BOOT
Cut 1**

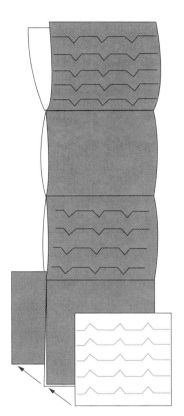

Pin the layers first, check the orientation, then sew.

Place a strip of Cowboy print with right side up on table.

Place a strip of appliqued Mink-y right side down with the bottom of the design at the seam.

Place a Cowboy strip right sides up on top of that.

Place a plain Red Mink-y strip wrong side up on top of that.

Align all edges. Pin the edge. Sew all 4 layers together as shown in the diagrams.

Flip the top and bottom pieces together so that all layers are right side out. Press.

Follow the diagram, adding the remaining rows.

Lightly press layers as you go.

Borders:

Square up edges of quilt. Pin the side borders in place.

Sew the side borders.

Press under ¼" edge of Mink-y border.

Fold the border strips in half towards back. Pin pressed edge to back of quilt.

Zig-zag stitch over the edge to secure.

Repeat for the other side.

Press under ¼" on each end of the top and bottom border strips.

Pin and sew following the steps for the side borders.

Hand stitch both ends closed.

Quilting:

Place stars on quilt as shown in photo. Pin and applique in place through all layers.

6. Continue stacking layers and sewing across bottom edges until you have seven bars of fabric.

Add Appliques

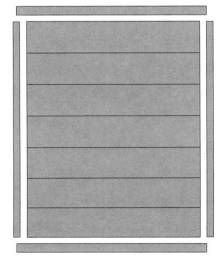

Blanket Assembly

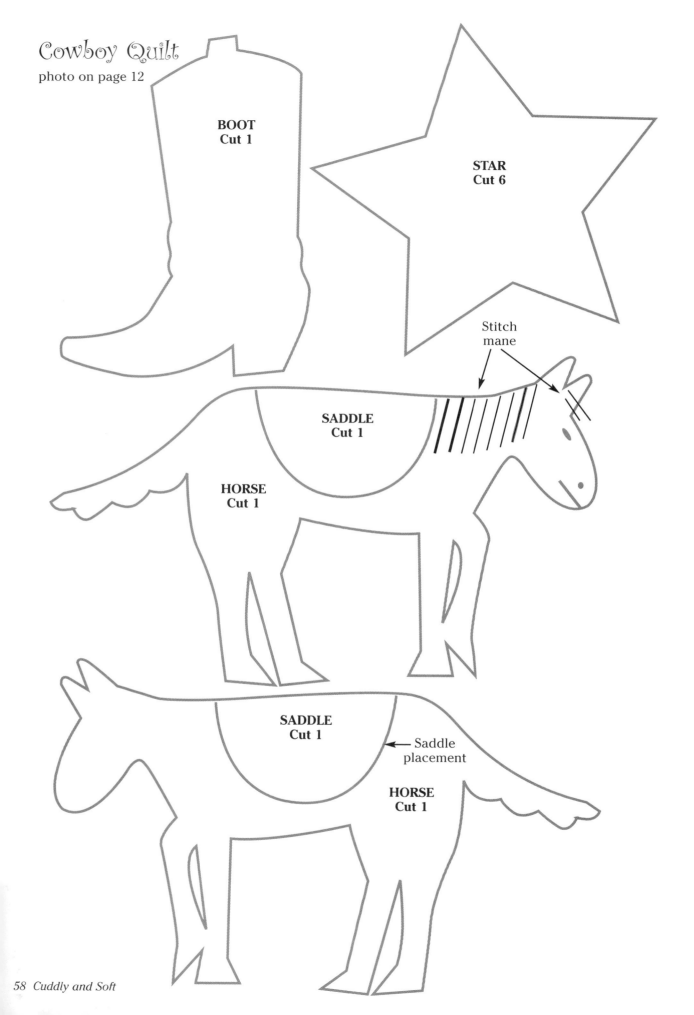

Cowboy Quilt
photo on page 12

BOOT
Cut 1

STAR
Cut 6

Stitch
mane

SADDLE
Cut 1

HORSE
Cut 1

SADDLE
Cut 1

Saddle
placement

HORSE
Cut 1

Christening Blankee

FINISHED SIZE: 30" x 39"

FABRICS:
¾ yard White Dots Mink-y Fleece
1 yard White chenille

MATERIALS:
2¾ yards ¾" wide soft lace
Needle and thread

CUTTING:
White Chenille:
 One 6½" square
 One 6½" x 22"
 One 6½" x 15½"
 One 31" x 40" for backing
White Dots Mink-y Fleece:
 Two 6½" x 30½"
 Two 6½" x 12½"
 Two 5¼" x 6½"
 Two 12½" x 15½"

INSTRUCTIONS:
All seam allowances are ¼".
Assembling top:
 Piece rows 2, 3 and 4 following the Assembly Diagram.
 Press seams open to avoid bulk.
 Sew the rows together. Press the seams open.
Backing:
 Place Blankee on Chenille backing with right sides together.
 Pin securely along all sides.
 Stitch around all sides, leaving a 6" opening to turn.
 Clip corners and turn right side out. Hand stitch opening closed. Press the edges.
 Topstitch ¼" from the edge.
Finishing:
 Pin lace around the perimeter of the cross.
 Pleat the lace to turn the corners.
 Machine stitch lace to the blankee through all layers.

6½" x 30½"

6½" x 12½" | 6½" X 6½" | 6½" x 12½"

5" X 6½" | 6½" x 22½" | 5" X 6½"

12½" x 15½" | 6½" X 15½" | 12½" x 15½"

6½" x 30½"

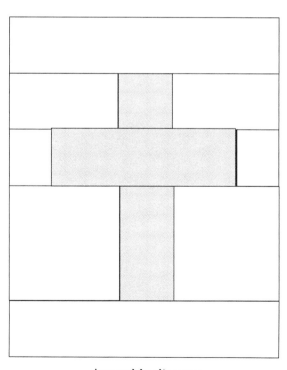

Assembly diagram

Pink Pillow
with Pom-Poms
photo on page 16

Pink Pillow with Pom Poms
FINISHED SIZE: 14" x 14"

FABRICS:
¼ yard Pink Mink-y Fleece
¼ yard Pink chenille
⅛ yard of 3 floral flannel fabrics

MATERIALS:
4 feet Pale Yellow pom-pom trim
12" pillow form
Needle and thread

CUTTING:
Four 6½" squares each of Mink-y and chenille
Ten 3" squares from each of 3 flannel fabrics (30 total)

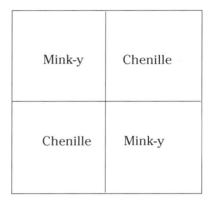

Four-Patch diagram

INSTRUCTIONS:
All seam allowances are ¼".
Piecing:
With right sides together, sew a Mink-y and chenille square together.
Press the seams open.
Make 4 sets.
Sew a 4-patch for the front and back of the pillow.
Flange:
Sew the flannel squares in a line 3" x 60".
Press the seams open.
Fold in half lengthwise and press.
Assembly:
Pin pom-pom trim to edge of pillow front.
Baste in place.
Align the raw edges of the flannel flange with the raw edges of the pillow front.
Pin and baste in place.
Backing:
Place pillow top, with flange and trim attached, right sides together with pillow back.
Stitch around all edges, leaving a 10" opening for turning.
Finishing:
Clip corners. Turn the pillow right sides out.
Insert pillow form.
Hand stitch opening closed.

Green Pillow
photo on page 7

Green Pillow
FINISHED SIZE: 10" x 16"

FABRICS:
⅓ yard Sage Mink-y Fleece
¼ yard Sage Floral flannel

MATERIALS:
24" Lavender Satin ribbon 1½" wide
24" Purple ribbon ½" wide
1½ yards Green fringe trim
Poly-Fil polyester stuffing
Needle and thread

CUTTING:
Two 10½" squares of Sage Mink-y
Four 3½" x 10½" of Floral flannel

Pillow diagram

INSTRUCTIONS:
All seam allowances are ¼".
Piecing:
With right sides together, sew a Floral piece to 2 opposite sides of each Mink-y square.
Press the seams open.
Ribbon:
Place Satin ribbon over the seam on right side of pillow front.
Stitch close to the edge along both sides of the ribbon.
Center the narrow ribbon on the Satin ribbon.
Stitch close to the edge along both sides of the ribbon. Repeat for other seam. Press lightly.
Fringe:
Pin fringe around the edge of the pillow top.
Baste in place.
Assembly:
With right sides together, pin the pillow front to the back.
Sew around the edges leaving a 4" opening for turning.
Finishing:
Clip corners. Turn the pillow right sides out.
Add stuffing.
Hand stitch opening closed.

Nine Patch Frog Blankee

FINISHED SIZE: 30" x 30"

FABRICS:
⅓ yard of Yellow Mink-y Fleece
⅔ yard of Yellow flannel with frog print
1 yard of Yellow chenille

MATERIALS:
DeNami Design Daisy rubber stamp
8" ribbon ⅜" wide
DMC Yellow embroidery floss
Needle and thread
Iron, Ironing board

CUTTING:
Four 10½" squares of flannel
Five 10½" squares of Mink-y Fleece
One 30½" square of chenille for the back.

INSTRUCTIONS:
All seam allowances ¼".

Pocket Pattern:
Use the pattern to cut out a pocket from chenille and one from flannel.

Emboss Mink-y:
Place a rubber stamp on ironing board, rubber side up. Place Mink-y fabric on top of rubber stamp with the right side facing the rubber. Mist lightly with water. Press a hot iron on fabric over the rubber stamp. Press firmly for fifteen seconds. Repeat steps for each flower. Please note that embossing will fade with repeated washings.

Assemble top:
Sew the following rows. See photo.
Row 1: Mink-y, Frog flannel, Mink-y.
Row 2: Frog flannel, Mink-y, Frog flannel.
Row 3: Same as Row 1.
Press seams open to avoid bulk.
Sew the rows together. Press the seams open.

Pocket:
Stitch decorative ribbon on chenille pocket 1" below top edge.
Place chenille and flannel pocket pieces right sides together.
Stitch around all sides leaving a 3" opening for turning.
Clip corners. Turn right side out and press.
Place finished pocket on pieced blankee top.
Be sure to leave some "ease" in pocket so the toy will fit.
Pin in place and topstitch along sides and bottom ¼" from the pocket edge.

Backing:
Place Blankee on Chenille backing with right sides together.
Pin securely along all sides. Stitch around all sides, leaving a 6" opening to turn.
Clip corners and turn right side out. Hand stitch opening closed.
Press the edges. Topstitch ¼" from the edge.

Finishing:
Tie the quilt layers together with 3 strands of embroidery floss.
From top, insert needle into blankee, pull floss through, leaving a 3" tail on top.
Insert needle into back of blankee, pull needle and floss through to top.

Tie floss in a double knot, trim ends as desired.
Make 3 evenly spaced ties along each seam between blocks.
Tie 5 times inside each quilt block in a pattern of a number 5 domino or die.

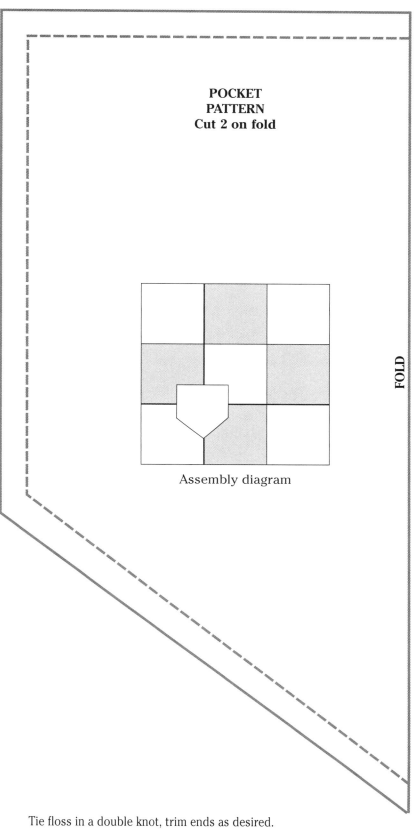

POCKET
PATTERN
Cut 2 on fold

Assembly diagram

FOLD

Funny Froggie Toy

photo on page 67

Funny Froggie

FINISHED SIZE: 7" x 11½"

FABRICS:
⅓ yard Green Mink-y Fleece
6" square Green cotton for belly
2" square White felt or fleece for eyes
1" square Black felt or fleece for pupil

MATERIALS:
Poly-Fil fiberfill stuffing,
Sulky rayon thread for applique and mouth
   (Black, White, Dark Green, Light Green)
Sulky self-adhesive Tear Away stabilizer
12" ribbon ⅜" wide
Needle and thread

CUTTING:
2 frog bodies from Green Mink-y
Belly applique from
   Green cotton
Eyes and pupils
   from felt or fleece

INSTRUCTIONS:
All seam allowances are ¼".
Face:
   Place eyes on face where
indicated.
   Adhere stabilizer on wrong side
of Mink-y behind eye placement.
   Use rayon thread to applique.
   Place pupil in lower part of eye. Applique.
   Stitch mouth as shown using wide zig-zag stitch.
   Go over mouth stitching 3 times so stitching
shows above nap of Mink-y.
   Remove excess stabilizer. Lightly press on wrong
side of face area.

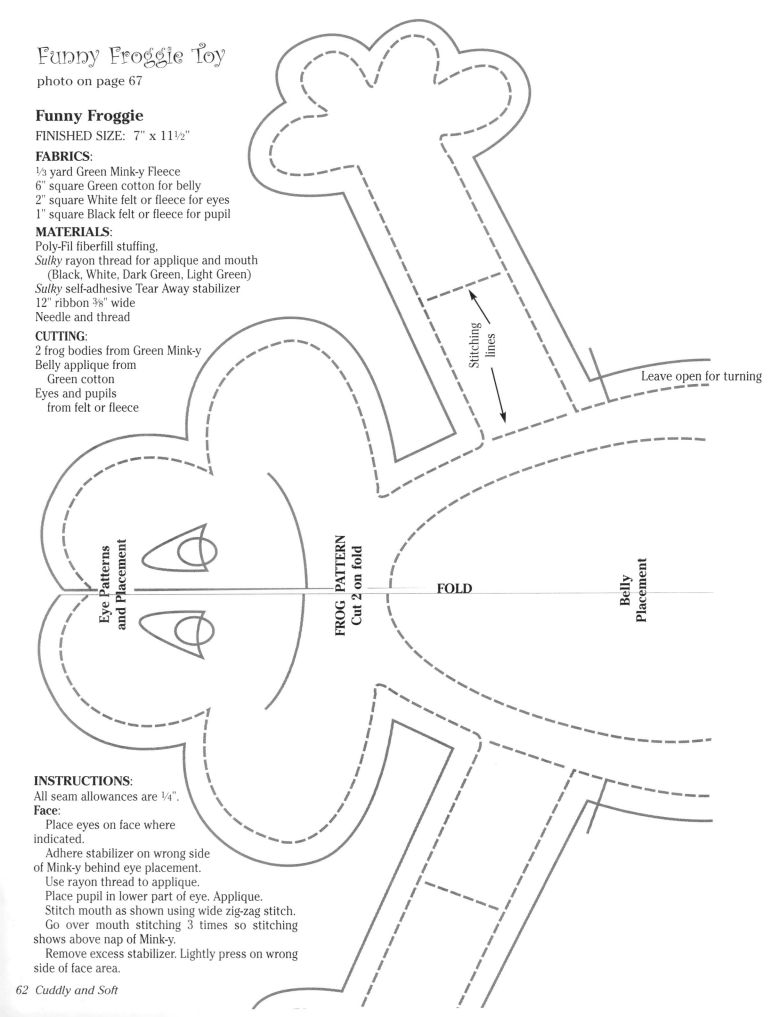

Stitching lines

Leave open for turning

Eye Patterns and Placement

FROG PATTERN Cut 2 on fold

FOLD

Belly Placement

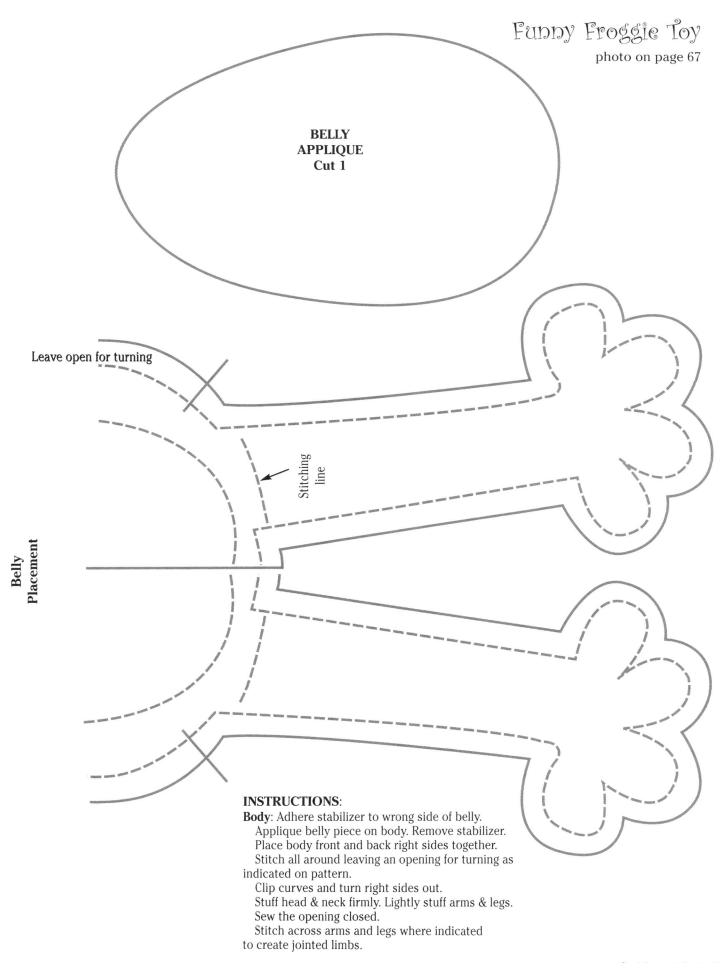

**BELLY
APPLIQUE
Cut 1**

Leave open for turning

Stitching line

Belly Placement

INSTRUCTIONS:

Body: Adhere stabilizer to wrong side of belly.
  Applique belly piece on body. Remove stabilizer.
  Place body front and back right sides together.
  Stitch all around leaving an opening for turning as
indicated on pattern.
  Clip curves and turn right sides out.
  Stuff head & neck firmly. Lightly stuff arms & legs.
  Sew the opening closed.
  Stitch across arms and legs where indicated
to create jointed limbs.

Basic Steps for Making
a Quilt or Blankee

Piecing the Top:

Follow placement diagram for assembly order. To join squares, place 2 fabrics right sides together and stitch together using ¼" seam allowance. Press seams open. Join rows together to form the quilt top. Square up edges after the top is fully assembled.

Layering:

It is not necessary to put batting in a Mink-y blankee.

Technique for No Binding Needed:

Place the quilt top right sides together with the back. Pin edges. Stitch together, leaving 6" opening for turning. Clip corners, turn right sides out. Gently press edges. Topstitch ¼" around perimeter.

Technique with Binding:

Layer the quilt top and back with wrong sides together. Baste and quilt as desired. Follow the instructions for binding.

Applique Quilting Technique:

Prepare the quilt layers using the No Binding Technique. Cut out shapes such as stars, circles, or squares from Mink-y fabric. Place them on the quilt leaving about 4" between the shapes. Pin in place. Applique through all layers around all edges using Sulky rayon thread. Sulky variegated thread adds a fun effect to your quilt.

Stipple... Machine Quilting:

Pin layers together every 4". Drop the feed dogs in your sewing machine and reduce the upper thread tension. Use large stipple quilting motion to free-motion quilt through the layers.

Machine Quilting:

Use a walking foot to quilt all layers together. To quilt "in the ditch", follow the seam lines. To quilt a grid pattern, use a chalk or water erasable pen to mark a grid on the quilt top. Then sew on the lines. Remove the markings.

Tie Your Quilt:

Tie the quilt layers together with 3 strands of embroidery floss. From top, insert needle into blankee, pull floss through, leaving a 3" tail on top. Insert needle into the back of blankee and pull the needle and floss through to the top. Tie floss in a surgeon's knot and trim the ends as desired. The quilt should be tied at least every 4". You may tie more closely if desired.

Binding:

Cut 2" wide strips and join the strips together at angles to reduce bulk. Fold one long side down ¼" to form a hem. Fold binding in half lengthwise. Align raw edges of binding with raw edges of quilt top and quilt back. Pin all around the blankee. Where the ends meet, tuck the raw end into the folded end. Stitch through all layers all around blankee. Fold the binding to back and hand stitch in place.

Surgeon's Knot

1. Begin with 2 working ends and wind one over the other.

2. Tuck right-hand end over and under the left-hand end.

3. Make second tuck with the left-hand end.

4. Pull tight to make the finished knot.

Embroidery Stitches

Working with Floss.

Separate embroidery floss.

Use 24" lengths of floss

Use a #8 embroidery needle.

Use 2 ply floss for the small details on some items.

Use 2 to 3 ply floss to outline large elements of the design and for larger and more stylized patterns.

Use 6 ply floss for eyes and mouths on large items.

Pay attention to backgrounds.

When working with lighter-colored fabrics, do not carry dark flosses across large unworked background areas. Stop and start again to prevent unsightly 'ghost strings' from showing through the front.

Another option is to back pale Mink-y or Chenille with a layer of muslin before you add embroidery stitches. This will help keep 'ghost strings' from showing.

Blanket Stitch

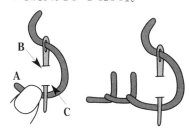

Come up at A, hold the thread down with your thumb, go down at B. Come back up at C with the needle tip over the thread. Pull the stitch into place. Repeat, outlining with the bottom legs of the stitch. Use this stitch to edge fabrics.

Chain Stitch

Come up at A. To form a loop, hold the thread down with your thumb, go down at B (as close as possible to A). Come back up at C with the needle tip over the thread. Repeat to form a chain.

Cross Stitch

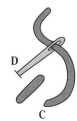

Make a diagonal Straight stitch (up at A, down at B) from upper right to lower left. Come up at C and go down at D to make another diagonal Straight stitch the same length as the first one. The stitch will form an X.

French Knot

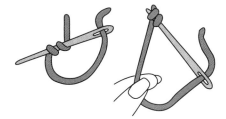

Come up at A. Wrap the floss around the needle 2 to 3 times. Insert the needle close to A. Hold the floss and pull the needle through the loops gently.

Running Stitch

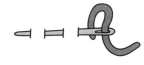

Come up at A. Weave the needle through the fabric, making short, even stitches. Use this stitch to gather fabrics, too.

Satin Stitch

Work small straight stitches close together and at the same angle to fill an area with stitches. Vary the length of the stitches as required to keep the outline of the area smooth.

Stem Stitch

Work from left to right to make regular, slanting stitches along the stitch line. Bring the needle up above the center of the last stitch. Also called 'Outline' stitch.

Straight Stitch

Come up at A and go down at B to form a simple flat stitch. Use this stitch for hair for animals and for simple petals on small flowers.

Back Stitch

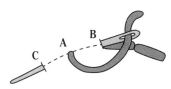

Come up at A, go down at B. Come back up at C. Repeat.

Frog Blankee & Toy

This blankee is ready to go with its fun frog toy in the pocket.

Drop it on the floor and it becomes a great play mat.

Take it in the car so Mr. Frog can incite your child's imagination when you travel.

The blankee is so snuggle soft, your child may even cuddle up for a nap on the way to Grandma's house with this new favorite!

instructions on pages 80 - 82

SUPPLIERS -
Most craft and variety stores carry an excellent assortment of supplies. If you need something special, ask your local store to contact the following companies.
Microfiber Polyester fabrics:
AvLyn 'Oh So Soft '
    866-564-5426, New York, NY
Benartex 'Minkee'
    212-840-3250, New York, NY
Moda 'Snuggles'
    972-484-8901, Dallas, TX
Materials and tools:
DMC Corp floss
    973-589-0606, S. Kearny, NJ
Fairfield Processing batting, PolyFil
    800-243-0989, Danbury, CT
Offray ribbon
    800-344-5533, Hagerstown, MD
Sulky of America thread
    800-874-4115, Port Charlotte, FL

MANY THANKS to my friends for their cheerful help and wonderful ideas!
Kathy McMillan
Jennifer Laughlin
Janie Ray • Janet Long
Donna Kinsey
David & Donna Thomason

Tips and Tricks for Working with Mink-y Type Fabrics

Mink-y sews and appliques like a dream. Mink-y can be combined with an endless variety of fabrics for stunning results. Experiment with chenille, flannel, cotton, polar fleece, felt, ribbon, upholstery trims and fibers for interesting and fun projects. Some projects call for face pieces cut from polar fleece or felt. Either can be used with success.

Read these tips before starting your project to ensure your success and beautiful results.

- Pre-wash: Be sure to pre-wash natural fiber fabrics you will be using with Mink-y.

- Mink-y will not shrink but cotton, flannel and chenille might if you fail to pre-wash it.

- Cutting: Be mindful of nap direction and stretch direction when placing pattern the pieces.

- The term "square up" means to trim edges evenly before proceeding to next step.

- Fringe: Fringe is best made using polar fleece since it is the same on both sides.

- The reverse side of Mink-y is polyester and the fleece looks better for fringe.

- Stabilize: When stitching appliques it is important to stabilize the back of Mink-y.

- I recommend Sulky self-adhesive tear away stabilizer.

- Small pieces of stabilizer are easier to remove if you lightly moisten the back.

- Pin, pin, pin! Mink-y is a little slippery.

- Slippage and distortion can be minimized by taking the time to pin securely before stitching. If you don't pin, it will be more likely to stretch as you sew.

- Mink-y may try to curl slightly on edges. Careful pinning will help control the curling.

- Sewing: Use universal size 80/12 sewing machine needles.

- Do NOT sew over pins. Remove them as you stitch.

- For applique, match the thread color to the piece you are stitching.

- I prefer Sulky rayon thread for applique.

- It is not necessary to use batting in a Mink-y blankee.

- Use a walking foot for machine quilting like stitch-in-the-ditch or quilting a grid.

- Pressing: Press seams open to reduce bulk. This is especially important when combining Mink-y with chenille or polar fleece.

- Pressing should be done gently with NO steam.

- Be especially gentle when pressing Mink-y Dot fabric or you will iron out the Dots.

- Press appliques from the wrong side.

- If you must press from the front, use only the tip of the iron and a pressing cloth.

- Clean up: Clean up fuzzy bits with an adhesive lint roller.

- Remember to clean the lint out of your bobbin case when you change bobbins.

- Don't forget to remove the lint that has collected in the feed dogs.